SYNTHESIS

WERNER BLASER

SYNTHESIS

TEXTE UND COLLAGEN
TEXTS AND COLLAGES

BIRKHÄUSER

Content
Inhalt

Foreword
Vorwort

"archi-collages" by werner blaser

werner blaser explores, collects and developes constantly ideas. his passion is to produce books that follow a particular theme and provide unexpected insights into supposedly well-known subjects.

he names his latest works "archi-collages".

however, what is to be understood with this definition? first of all we take the term "collage": this conventionally refers to an artistic work consisting of one or several elements glued onto a base, usually made of cardboard or paper. the word derives from the french "coller" (to glue) and could in fact be applied to any work that is assembled by means of an adhesive. then, there is the word "archi": it derives from ancient greek and in werner blaser's life you find the term "architecture".

werner blaser is well known for his skilled architectural photographs which he presents in publications showing carefully selected juxtapositions. currently, his focus has shifted from such pictorial comparisons to a new type of artistic aesthetic. for werner blaser, an archi-collage needs to fulfill different criteria. in this context the photograph no longer merely communicates pictorial content, but is also a tool serving an artistic goal. the juxtaposed elements combine with one another to form a new entity – a process that werner blaser refers to as an "encounter." such encounters can occur as angular cuts, overlays and contrasts. there is no use of double exposures. along with their artistic claim, this is the new statement made by werner blaser's latest works.

the so realized pictures are accompanied by autobiographical texts. they tell from encounters with people, landscapes and buildings and these individual archi-collages, in turn, merge with his texts, creating an "archi-text-collage".

jakob bill august 2016

werner blasers archi-collagen

werner blaser forscht, sammelt und entwickelt unentwegt ideen. er liebt es bücher zu produzieren, die einem thema folgen und oft ungeahnte neue ausblicke auf vermeintlich bekanntes vermitteln.

archi-collagen nennt er seine jüngsten werke.

doch, was ist unter diesem begriff zu verstehen? zuerst einmal der einfachere begriff: unter einer *collage* verstehen wir üblicherweise ein künstlerisches werk. es ist aus einem oder mehreren teilen auf einer meist aus karton oder papier bestehenden unterlage auf- und zusammengeklebt. abgeleitet ist diese bezeichnung vom französischen *coller* (kleben) und könnte eigentlich für jegliche werke, die mittels klebstoff zusammengefügt sind, verwendet werden. dann *archi*: dieses wort ist vom griechischen abgeleitet und findet sich im leben von werner blaser im begriff *architektur* wieder.

bekannt ist werner blaser bereits für seine mit der kamera eingefangenen architekturaufnahmen. auch in publikationen hat er diese in ausgewogen gewählten gegenüberstellungen jeweils dem leser und betrachter dargebracht – aber es waren eben bildliche vergleiche! neu stellt er sich auch einer künstlerischen ästhetik. eine archi-collage hat also für werner blaser verschiedene bedingungen zu erfüllen. die fotografie hat nicht mehr nur einen bildvermittelnden auftrag, sie ist auch mittel zum künstlerischen zweck. die gegenüberstellungen verbinden sich so ineinander, dass sie sich zu einem neuen ganzen vereinen – werner blaser nennt dies auch eine *begegnung*. diese kann durch schräge schnitte, überlagerungen und kontraste erfolgen. die fotografische doppelbelichtung kommt nicht zur anwendung. dies ist – zusammen mit dem künstlerischen anspruch – die neue aussage von werner blaser.

die so erzielten bilder werden begleitet von texten autobiografischen inhalts. sie handeln sehr oft von begegnungen mit personen, landschaft und architektur und wieder stellt man fest, dass auch die einzelnen archi-collagen mit den entsprechenden texten sich zusammenfügen und zu einer archi-text-collage werden.

jakob bill august 2016

Setting Out

The Second World War, which took place during my youth, was a distressing experience. When the war came to an end in 1945, I was taking part in a Swiss army refresher course and was permitted to celebrate the newfound peace in Endingen Church in Aargau. At last, borders were open again and we could hope to complete our education abroad. My first forays outside Switzerland took me to nearby Alsace and Baden. However, I was already planning to venture to more distant lands.

In the spring of 1948, as a 24-year-old, I travelled through northern Italy, visiting Milan, Ravenna, and Venice. At the time, journeying by rail often meant sitting on a bench in a cargo carriage and adapting to these kinds of situations was an early and important learning process. Coping on your own requires an understanding of the world in its reality.

My experience of the wider world began in summer 1948 with little preparation and few contacts. I decided to travel through Scandinavia. My bicycle was my trusty and money-saving companion, whilst my sketchbooks were part of my luggage from the onset. I was eager to put into practice the freehand drawing technique I had learned at the Basel School of Design. My destinations were Copenhagen, Stockholm, and Oslo, and I spent three months in each city. I had set myself the task of making accurate drawings of furniture displayed in the museums there and the results filled several sketchbooks. It was during this time that I began to gain an understanding of the past and to draw conclusions from it relating to the present. The impressive objects I encountered never struck me as being foreign. Secular building and its origins in this part of the world provided me with important examples of the integration of function, material, and form and the role played by climate, topography, and national character. The challenge was to recognize the problems presented by wood in terms of construction and design, to reconceive them, and to resolve them with new ideas.

My first encounter with Copenhagen's great architecture occurred in 1949 as a consequence of an exchange of books with the pioneering architect Paul Artaria, a man who helped to shape Swiss modernism, who was one of my teachers in Basel. Artaria was also kind enough to introduce me to members of the Danish architectural elite. This included my acquaintance with the architect Steen Eiler Rasmussen, with whom I discussed the Buddha's sitting position, unaware at the time that it was a theme I would explore in some detail in future years. Such encounters are the food of life; without personal relationships spanning the globe, architecture would be reduced to empty gestures. But how do we create such encounters? An encounter requires openness and adaptation; it is a process of simultaneously giving and taking. Through this process a dialog is created that needs to be cultivated long before it can be communicated in a book.

Auftakt – zur Sache

Der Zweite Weltkrieg während meiner Jugendjahre war eine bedrückende Erfahrung. Als 1945 der Krieg zu Ende ging, war ich als Schweizer Soldat im Wiederholungskurs und durfte mit Kollegen in der Kirche im aargauischen Endingen den Frieden einläuten. Endlich wieder offene Grenzen und die Hoffnung, die Lehre im Ausland zu vervollständigen! Ins nahegelegene Elsass und in die badische Nachbarschaft führten mich die ersten Schritte ins Ausland. Doch auch fernere Länder waren schon in Sichtweite.

Schon im Frühling 1948 reiste ich als 24-Jähriger durch Oberitalien zu den Städten Mailand, Ravenna und Venedig. Damals gab es nur Bahnfahrten in Güterwagen auf Bänken. Das Sichanpassen an solche Notsituationen war ein erster wichtiger Lernprozess: Es braucht ein Verständnis für die Welt, wie sie ist, wenn man in ihr bestehen will.

Mein Weg in die große Welt begann dann im Sommer 1948 mit wenig Vorbereitungen oder Beziehungen: Ich wollte Skandinavien bereisen! Das Fahrrad war mein treuer und ökonomischer Begleiter, aber auch Skizzenhefte gehörten zum Gepäck. Das an der Kunstgewerbeschule in Basel gelernte Freihandzeichnen sollte ja in die Praxis umgesetzt werden. Ziel waren die Städte Kopenhagen, Stockholm und Oslo, in denen ich mich dann jeweils drei Monate aufgehalten habe. Die Aufgabe, die ich mir stellte, war, in den dortigen Volksmuseen Möbelaufnahmen in Maß und Zeichnung festzuhalten. Mehrere Skizzenbücher wurden mit diesen Objekten gefüllt. So habe ich gelernt, das Vergangene zu verstehen und daraus Schlüsse für die Gegenwart zu ziehen. Nie kamen mir diese beeindruckenden Objekte fremd vor. Der profane Hausbau und dessen Ursprung waren wichtige Beispiele für die Integration von Funktion, Material und Gestalt, bei der zugleich auch Klima, Topologie und Volkscharakter eine Rolle spielten. Die Aufgabe war, die gestalterischen und konstruktiven Probleme von Holzobjekten zu erkennen, zu durchdenken und mit neuen Impulsen zu lösen.

Meine erste Begegnung mit der großen Architektur in Kopenhagen hatte ich 1949 als Folge eines Austausches von Büchern mit meinem Fachlehrer, dem Pionierarchitekten Paul Artaria aus Basel. Er prägte nicht nur die schweizerische Moderne, sondern öffnete mir auch den Weg, die damalige Elite dänischer Architekten zu kontaktieren. Dazu gehörte auch der Architekt Steen Eiler Rasmussen, mit dem ich dann über die Sitzstellung Buddhas sprach, nicht wissend, dass sie später zu einem meiner Themen werden würde. Begegnung ist wahres Leben. Ohne weltweite persönliche Beziehungen würde Architektur zur leeren Geste. Aber wie begegnen? Begegnung verlangt Offenheit und Anpassung, ist Geben und Nehmen zugleich. So bildet sich ein Gegenüber, das gepflegt werden muss, lange bevor es dann in Büchern vermittelt werden kann.

Taking measurements, National Museum Helsinki
Seating and foot elements made from a tree trunk
(photo: Claudia Neuenschwander)
Sketch: Werner Blaser, 1953

Maßaufnahmen National Museum Helsinki
Sitz- und Fußteile aus einem Baumstamm gefertigt
(Foto: Claudia Neuenschwander)
Skizze: Werner Blaser, 1953

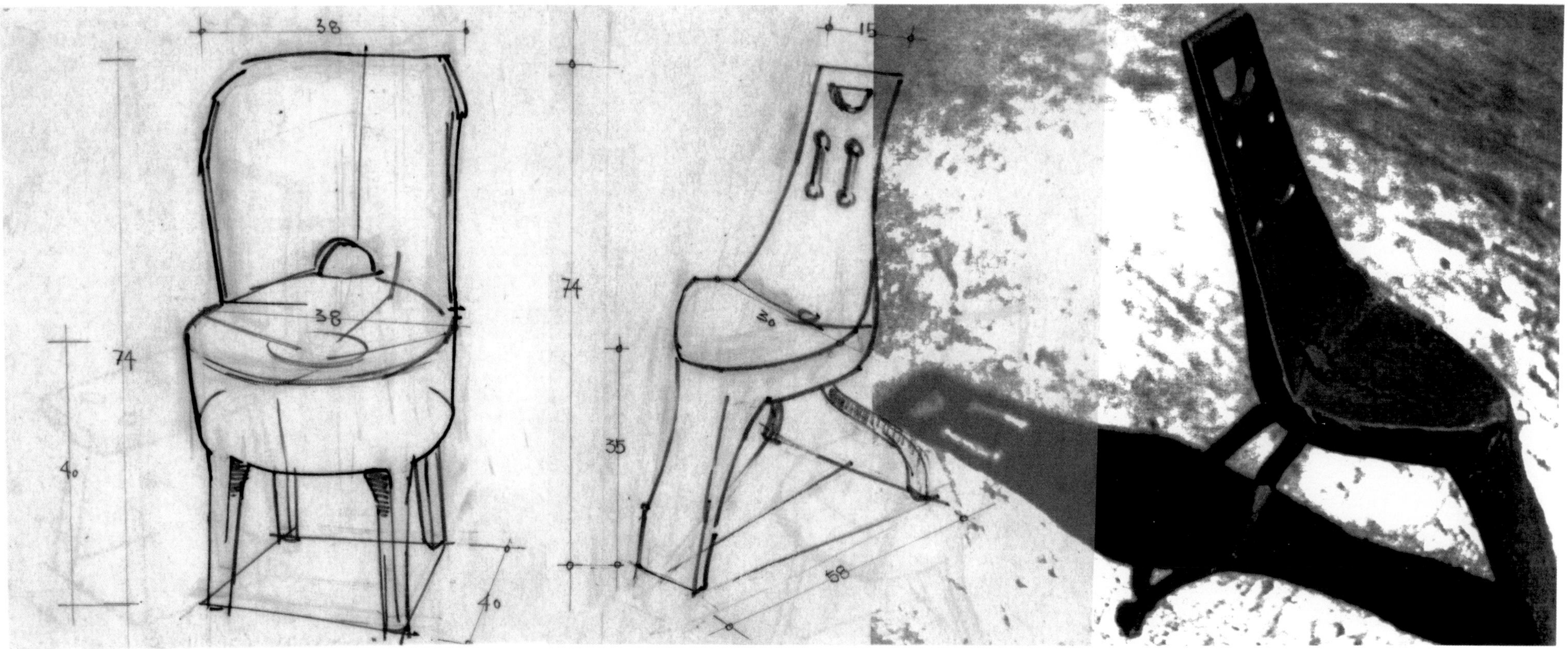
38
74
38
40
40
15
74
30
35
58

Seeing – Thinking – Understanding

During my wanderings, relationships formed – mediated and cultivated in constant dialog and in constant engagement with the legacy of modernism. This experience of concrete and personal proximity moved me again and again, investing my life with purpose. When reflecting on this evolved network of relationships, I am still moved by what a gift they have been.

I was not interested in indulging vices or squandering my time during my journeys, devoting myself instead to seeing, thinking, and gaining understanding. All my energies went into absorbing and processing what I experienced. I was intent on using my time productively, on being open to everything new, and finding the truly viable qualities within each new experience. Every architect, of course, wants to create a new "world": a building is always a unique object charged with atmosphere. Already as a little boy I built huts using cloths in our garden. Such spaces provide an important experience for the development of a sense of self, encapsulating both continuity and change.

Architects are children of culture; they are technically orientated and culturally connective. They travel to the arenas of history in order to discover the architectural secrets of past cultures and experience them up close, guided by a desire for intensive images, insights, and meaning. In this way, high-quality architecture becomes visible and comprehensible.

Sehen – Denken – Verstehen

Während meiner Wanderschaft haben sich Beziehungen aufgebaut. Im stetigen Dialog vermittelt und gepflegt, in stetiger Auseinandersetzung mit dem Erbe der Moderne. Diese sachliche und persönliche Nähe zu erfahren, berührte mich und gab mir immer wieder neuen Lebenssinn. Es ist für mich noch immer ein Geschenk, sich dieses gewachsene Netz an Beziehungen vor Augen zu führen.

Auf den großen Reisen hatten Laster und Herumhängen bei mir keine Chance. Stattdessen widmete ich mich dem Sehen, Denken und Verstehen. Meine ganze Kraft ging ins Aufnehmen und Aufarbeiten. Es galt, ohne Zeitverschleiß für alles Neue offen zu sein und darin die wirklich tragfähigen Eigenschaften aufzudecken. Jeder Architekt will doch eine neue „Welt" erschaffen: Ein Bau ist immer ein mit Atmosphäre aufgeladenes Unikat. Schon als Bub baute ich im Familiengarten Hütten aus Tüchern, denn der eigens gebaute Hüttenraum ist eine wichtige Erfahrung für die Entwicklung des Ich-Seins. Darin liegen Kontinuität und Wandel zugleich.

Architekten sind Kinder der Kultur, sie sind technisch orientiert und kulturell anschlussfähig. Sie reisen zu den Schauplätzen der Geschichte, um die konstruktiven Geheimnisse vergangener Kulturen zu entdecken und hautnah zu erleben, geleitet von einer Sehnsucht nach intensiven Bildern und Erkenntnissen, nach Sinn. So wird gute Architektur sicht- und begreifbar.

Southern China: Moon gate as passage and doorway (photo 1980)
Mies van der Rohe: Farnsworth House, Plano, Illinois, USA, 1945–1950 (photo 1952)

Südchina: Mondtor als Durchgang und Öffnung (Foto 1980)
Mies van der Rohe: Farnsworth House, Plano, Illinois, USA, 1945–1950 (Foto 1952)

Finland's Primal Natural Environment

My first really significant travel experience after completing carpentry and draftsmen apprenticeship in Basel was my encounter with the great architect Alvar Aalto in Finland. In hindsight, this contact, together with the eighteen months I spent working in Helsinki, constituted an ideal point of departure for the development of a committed young explorer such as myself. Being involved in the development of furniture in the context of building construction means working on the scale of the smallest self-contained unit of human living space.

For the first time in my professional life I was participating in the realization of an overall concept that integrated architecture and furniture. Even today, the technological possibilities of wood as an organic construction material have still not been exhausted. The vast forests of Finland are a source of this remarkable raw material. Aalto's product design was founded on basic research into the structures of wood. He developed a structural component in which the horizontal and vertical functions are unified in a single element. The bending process he devised involves a systematic splitting of the wood, i.e. saw-cuts into which pieces of wood veneer are inserted and glued to create a series of layers. The last phase of Aalto's ongoing development of this process entailed the widening of a solid piece of wood to form a unified surface. When used as a base, such elements no longer require the screw used in the various stool supports characteristic of Aalto's earlier work. These stages of development clearly illustrate how bending wood generates changes in the overall form. Between 1949 and 1951, I had the opportunity to learn by doing: to experience, as Aalto taught me, the generation of a product design from an experiment. The new furniture types that he developed with his firm Artek (art and technology) were devised in the context of furnishing schemes for entire buildings.

However, it was not only Aalto's intellectual vitality, but also the harmony between human being and landscape that forged the bond I feel with the most remote land in northern Europe. On subsequent journeys through the forests of North Karelia, I became aware of how architecture and nature condition one another. The primal form of the expansive lakes in this part of the world forms a tension with the vertical structure of the forests. A curved line is the spontaneous expression of the dynamic that is reflected in this landscape of forests and lakes.

A particular experience in Central Finland showed me the truth that lies in the natural environment. In the forest around Alvar and Elissa Aalto's summerhouse on the island of Muuratsalo in Lake Päijänne, the squabbling between my two grandchildren Till and Mia simply ceased. The natural environment helps to heal; one needs to grasp its impact, absorb it, and let go.

Since then, the way I see and experience the world internally, my attentiveness has been oriented to seeking the objective truth of material and structure, and of proportion and space. It is not "isms" that inspire meaningful architecture, but the sense of fulfillment that is triggered in us when a simple object assumes meaning for us based on its essential form and elegant proportions.

In the Nordic forests and lake country, a kind of awakening is celebrated. Here, even that which has died becomes radiant. The effects of the last ice age are evident everywhere in the meager soil and the glacial boulders. In the world of the forest, one learns to see anew and this experience shapes us intellectually in a particular way. A section of forest floor, with its scent, colors, and play of light, becomes its own Eden. As an integral environment for the people of northern Europe, the forest is an essential element of cultural life there. It is both a legacy of their grandfathers and an inheritance for their children. Punctured through with sun and moonlight, it radiates peace and tranquility throughout the year.

The image of bright summer nights and of the endless sunsets with gleaming oceans of color becomes a myth that reaches deep into the soul. The constant change in this paradise of nature lends people a self-composure, gives them hope, a sense of peace, and confidence in life. The human as subject and nature as object become one. As Goethe said, "It is the fresh air of the open field where we belong by right: It is as if the spirit of God there breathes immediately upon men and thereby a godlike strength exercises its influence over him."

Ur-Natur Finnland

Mein erstes großes Reiseerlebnis nach der Handwerks- und Zeichnerlehre in Basel war die Begegnung mit dem damaligen großen Architekten Alvar Aalto in Finnland. Im Nachhinein war dieser Kontakt, zusammen mit der eineinhalbjährigen Arbeit in Helsinki, ein ausgezeichneter Ausgangspunkt für die seriöse Entwicklung eines jungen Suchenden. Sich mit Möbelentwicklungen zu beschäftigen, ist, im strukturellen Zusammenhang mit dem Bau, als die kleinste in sich geschlossene Zelle des menschlichen Lebensraums zu betrachten.

Erstmals war ich in meinem Berufsleben an der Erarbeitung eines Gesamterscheinungsbildes von Architektur und Möbeln beteiligt. Als organischer Werkstoff ist Holz in seinen technologischen Möglichkeiten noch heute nicht erschöpft. Die riesigen finnischen Wälder liefern den Rohstoff. Aalto begann bei seiner Produktgestaltung mit der Grundlagenforschung zu Holzstrukturen. Er entwickelte ein Bauelement, in dem horizontale und vertikale Funktionen in einem Teil vereinigt sind. Das Biegeverfahren ist durch systematisches Aufspalten des Holzes gekennzeichnet, d. h. durch das Einsägen und Einsetzen von Holzfurnieren oder durch die Schichtenverleimung. Aaltos letzte Entwicklung dieses Verfahrens war die Verbreiterung eines massiven Holzstückes zur Fläche wie aus einem Guss. Bei derartigen Fußelementen ist die Schraube, wie sie bei den variablen Hockerunterstützungen der früheren Arbeiten Aaltos verwendet wurde, entbehrlich geworden. In diesen Stadien der Entwicklung wird der Formwandel auf dem Gebiet der Holzverformung deutlich sichtbar. Ich hatte von 1949 bis 1951 die Gelegenheit, durch Mitwirkung zu lernen: zu erleben, wie Aalto mich lehrte, aus dem Experiment eine Produktgestaltung zu vollenden. Die neuen Möbeltypen, die er dann mit seiner Firma Artek (Art und Technik) entwickelte, sind im Zusammenhang mit Gebäudemöblierungen entstanden.

Aber nicht nur die geistige Vitalität Aaltos, sondern auch die Harmonie von Mensch und Landschaft hat mich an das entlegenste Land im Norden von Europa gebunden. Auf meinen späteren Reisen durch die Wälder Nordkareliens wurde mir bewusst, wie Architektur und Natur sich gegenseitig bedingen: Die Urform der weiten Seen steht in Spannung zur Vertikalgliederung der Wälder. Eine Kurvenlinie ist der spontane Ausdruck jener Dynamik, die sich in der Landschaft der Wälder und Seen widerspiegelt.

Ein Erlebnis in Mittelfinnland hat mir gezeigt, welche Wahrheit in der Natur liegt: Im Wald, beim Sommerhaus von Alvar und Elissa Aalto in Muuratsalo am Päijännesee, ist zwischen meinen beiden Enkelkindern Till und Mia jegliches Gezänk verstummt. Die Natur hilft heilen; man muss ihre Wirkung begreifen, annehmen und sich lösen lassen.

Mein Sehen und Erleben im inneren Ausdruck, meine Aufmerksamkeit ist seitdem auf die objektive Wahrheit von Stoff und Gefüge, von Maß und Raum ausgerichtet. Es sind keine Ismen, die das sinnerfüllte Bauen beflügeln, sondern es ist die Erfüllung, die sich bei uns einstellt, wenn ein einfaches Objekt aufgrund seiner inneren Gestalt und seiner geschaffenen Proportionen für uns Bedeutung annimmt.

In den nordischen Wäldern und Seenlandschaften wird eine Art Erweckung zelebriert. Dort kommt selbst das Verstorbene zum Leuchten. Überall sind die Auswirkungen der letzten Eiszeit im kargen Boden und an den Findlingen erkennbar. Man lernt in der Welt des Waldes mit anderen Augen sehen, was uns auf eigenartige Weise geistig prägt: Ein Stück Waldboden wird in Duft, Farbe und Lichtspiel zum eigenen Eden. Der Wald als zweites Zuhause ist für die Menschen im Norden Europas ein untrennbarer Teil ihres historischen Kulturlebens, er ist sowohl Erbe der Großväter als auch ein Darlehen für die Kinder. Vom Sonnen- und Mondlicht durchbrochen, strahlt er das ganze Jahr über Ruhe und Stille aus.

Das unendliche Bild der hellen Sommernächte, der ewige Sonnenuntergang mit seinem glühenden Farbenmeer wird zu einem Mythos, der tief in die Seele geht. Der stete Wandel in diesem Paradies der Natur verleiht den Menschen Gelassenheit, er gibt ihnen Hoffnung, Frieden und ein Leben mit Zuversicht. Subjekt Mensch und Objekt Natur werden eins. Bereits Goethe hat gesagt: „Die frische Luft des freien Feldes ist der einzige Ort, wo wir hingehören: Es ist, als ob der Geist Gottes dort den Menschen unmittelbar anwehte und eine göttliche Kraft ihren Einfluss ausübte."

Finland: Punkaharju lake landscape, Finnish Karelia Nature Reserve
Alvar Aalto: Iittala vases, first produced in 1937

Finnland: Seenlandschaft Punkaharju, Finnisch-Karelien (Naturdenkmal)
Alvar Aalto: Vasen von Iittala, seit 1937

Visions Take on Form

The wide world was opened up to me in Scandinavia and Finland. At that time I was not using a camera, only a pencil, which I took with me when visiting the open-air museums there. The expansive, open forests and the organically formed lakes with their "endless" horizon were at once great experiences and harbingers: I would never have thought that in 1951 my path would lead from Alvar Aalto in Helsinki to Amsterdam and from there, by ship, to the USA. Chicago, the Western "El Dorado" for early modern architecture and contemporary modernism thus became my "adopted home." So much of what came thereafter was shaped by Chicago: my attitude, my learning to truly see, and my understanding of good architecture. This experienced truth was so powerful that it continues to shape my thinking to this day.

My optimistic nature helped me to be open to see things differently and to experience them in a new way. To intimate the world in its entirety is at once a realization and an obligation. Comprehending and understanding are the roots of action; they shape our fundamental tenets and thereby our architectural principles, including our approach to structure and material. With its possibilities and limits, visible construction is a central aspect of honest design. Natural materials that facilitate design have a particular expressive value. Distinctive characteristics are invested in materials: stone organizes, wood forms, and metal nurtures. The selected material is the raw material (derived from the Latin word "mater" or mother) for the stimulating beauty of the texture. Its aesthetic is the manifestation of its external sensuous perception: as solid, concrete form.

The organizing principle of my life has been the constant search for new horizons. Independent of the hectic world and without preconception, I have always sought truth. Architecture always needs to be discovered anew: in its own right and for others. At the same time that which endures needs to be absorbed by the mind and be preserved. Traversing such a path requires persistence; it demands a great deal of energy and a good constitution. Nevertheless, talking is not acting! Work is sustained activity. One reacts to time, which never stands still. Those capable of development remain partners of their contemporaries. It helps to have a strong will that enables you time and again to gather your strength, to create something new, and to make more out of our life. It is only in this way that my youthful dreams have become reality during the course of my working life.

Visionen nehmen Gestalt an

Eröffnet wurde mir die weite Welt in Skandinavien und Finnland. Damals kannte ich den Fotoapparat noch nicht – nur den Zeichenstift, der mich auch in die dortigen Freilichtmuseen begleitete. Die weiten, offenen Wälder und die organisch geformten Seen mit ihrem „endlosen" Horizont waren große Erlebnisse und Vorboten zugleich: Nie hätte ich zu glauben gewagt, dass mich mein Weg 1951 von Alvar Aalto in Helsinki nach Amsterdam und von dort mit dem Studentenschiff in die USA führen würde. Chicago, das westliche „El Dorado" für frühe moderne Architektur und aktuelle Moderne, wurde so auch meine „Wahlheimat". Vieles, was danach kam, war geprägt von Chicago: meine Haltung, mein Sehenlernen, mein Verstehen von guter Architektur. Diese erlebte Wahrheit war so stark, dass sie bis heute anhält.

Positives Denken war für mich immer ein Chance, Dinge anders zu sehen und in neuer Weise erfahrbar zu machen. Die Welt in ihrer Ganzheit zu erahnen, ist eine Erkenntnis und eine schöne Verpflichtung zugleich. Begreifen und Verstehen sind Wurzeln unseres Handelns, prägen unsere wesentlichen Grundsätze, somit auch unsere Architekturprinzipien wie etwa Konstruktion und Material. Sichtbares Konstruieren ist in seinen Möglichkeiten und Grenzen ein zentraler Faktor ehrlicher Gestaltung. Natürliche Materialien, die ein gutes Gestalten ermöglichen, haben immer einen besonderen Ausdruckswert. Im Material sind markante Eigenschaften angelegt: Stein ordnet, Holz formt, und Metall erzieht. Das erlesene Material ist der Grundstoff („mater"/ Mutter) für die belebende Schönheit der Textur. Ihre Ästhetik ist die Form der äußeren sinnlichen Wahrnehmung: als anschauliche Gestalt.

Die Lehre meines Lebens: der stete Aufbruch zu neuen Horizonten. Unabhängig von der hektischen Welt und ohne irgendwelches Ansinnen, suchte ich immer das Wahre. Architektur ist immer wieder neu zu entdecken: für sich wie für die Anderen; zugleich ist Bleibendes im Geiste aufzunehmen und zu bewahren. Um diesen Weg zu bestreiten, braucht man Beständigkeit; er verlangt viel Energie und eine gute Verfassung. Dennoch: Reden ist nicht machen! Arbeiten ist fortgesetzte Aktivität. Man reagiert auf die Zeit, die nie stillsteht. Ist man entwicklungsfähig, bleibt man auch ein Partner seiner Zeitgenossen. Ein starker Wille hilft dabei, sich immer wieder aufzuraffen, Neues zu kreieren und mehr aus unserem Leben zu machen. Nur so sind in meinem Arbeitsleben die Jugendträume allesamt Wirklichkeit geworden!

Mies van der Rohe: Bacardi building, Santiago de Cuba, 1957–1959
Li Ming-chung: Treatise on Chinese architecture, 12th century

Mies van der Rohe: Bacardi-Gebäude in Santiago de Cuba, Projekt 1957–1959
Li Ming-chung: Abhandlung über Architektur in China, 12. Jahrhundert

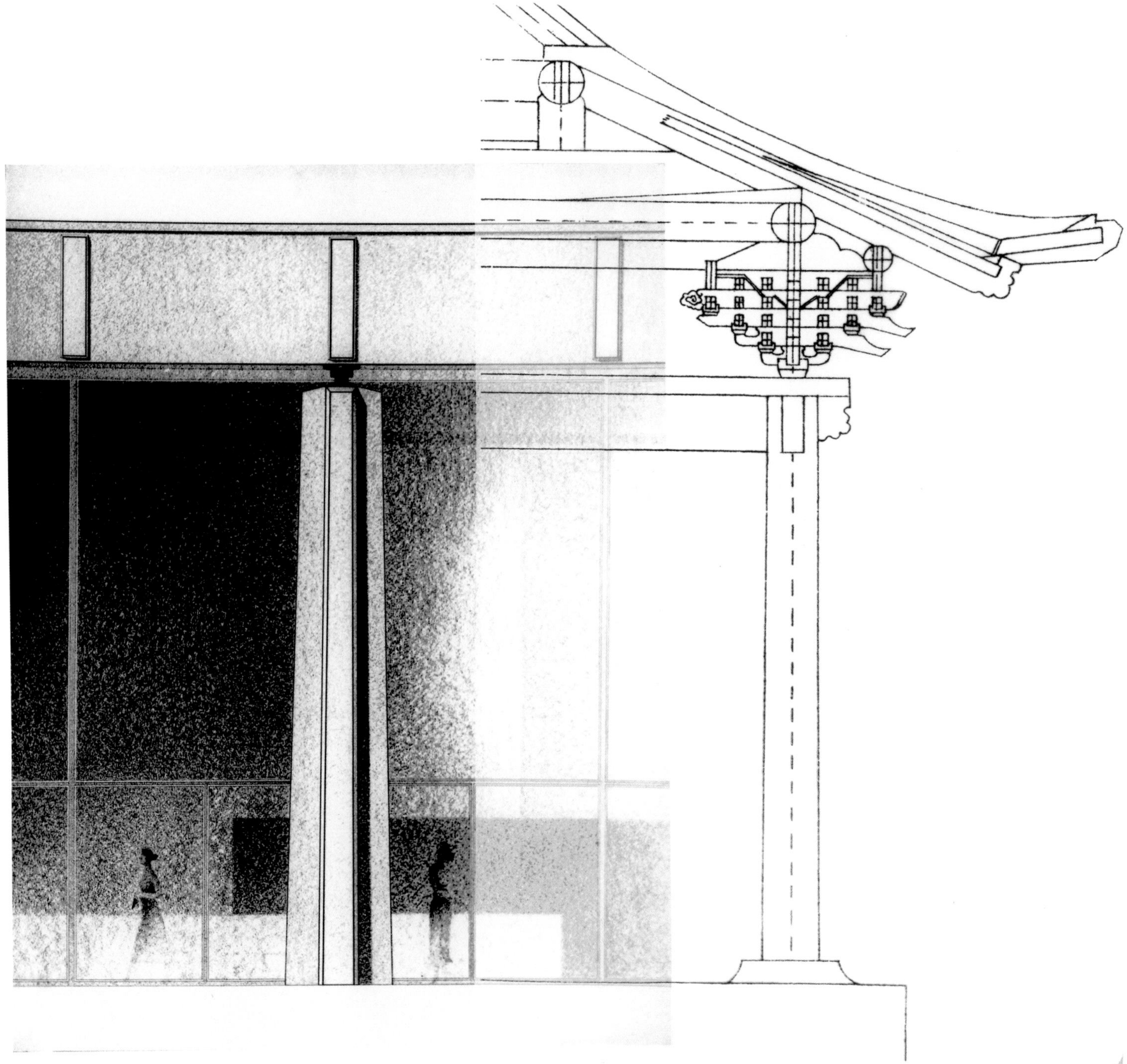

Chicago, the El Dorado of Modern Architecture

My early encounter with architecture was broadened during my two-year sojourn in Chicago between 1951 and 1953, during my studies at the Illinois Institute of Design, and while working for the Bauhaus architect Bertrand Goldberg. Among the acquaintances I made during this period in this veritable treasure trove of architects was Frank Lloyd Wright. I encountered him for the first time on the Chicago Loop walking along the street in a hat and frock coat and carrying a cane, and later at his summer school in Spring Green, Wisconsin, where the landscape recalls Japan.

Learning photography was also part of this initial phase, and I began to build up my photo archive documenting the work of Mies van der Rohe and the Chicago School of Architecture. Documenting and interpreting with my camera was to become a lifelong process. It began in 1951 during a photography course at the Illinois Institute of Design ("The Late Bauhaus of Moholy Nagy"), where we were given the task of creating a photogram. Aran Suskind, a professor at the Illinois Institute of Design, was an excellent photography teacher, indeed one of the world's best. With his help, I was able to purchase a Rolleicord, despite my lack of money. My first photos were of the Farnsworth House by Mies van der Rohe in Plano, Illinois, for which I received a positive review from the Museum of Modern Art in New York. A professor of architecture at the Institute of Design asked me whether the subject of my photographs was Japan. This was the first sign that pointed me towards the contemporary encounter between Far Eastern traditions and Western ideas.

For me, lending architecture photographs a poetic framework is the art of all truths that life reveals to us. Taking black-and-white photographs at all levels of illumination constitutes a way of seeing that reduces the pictorial motif to its essential elements. For me, discovering architecture with photos is an almost "religious" undertaking.

Chicago was also where I was properly introduced to Far Eastern architecture by the Changs, siblings from Shanghai: Pao-Chi, who had obtained a Master of Architecture under Mies van der Rohe at the Illinois Institute of Technology, and her brother Chao-Kang, who had obtained the same degree under Walter Gropius at Harvard University in Boston. My encounter with them marked the beginning of my exploration of the theme of "West meets East."

I completed my first book, *Japanese Temples and Tea-Houses* in 1955. Based on my six-month trip to Japan, its theme was the classical Japanese pavilion and its contemporary significance. The way I perceived Japan was heavily influenced by Mies and to acknowledge this, I gave him a copy of the book. He then asked me for fifty more copies for his students and invited me to create a book about his own work. This subsequent book entitled, *Mies van der Rohe. The Art of Structure* was produced during the summer months of 1963 and 1964 in Chicago. The title was inspired by Paul Hindemith's essay on J. S. Bach, in which the author argues that with the "art of the fugue," Bach achieved the apex of his art. This could also be said of Mies during his period of work in Chicago between 1937 and 1969: with the truth of visible construction in steel and glass.

Chicago, das Eldorado für Architektur

Meine persönliche Begegnung mit der Architektur vervollständigte sich 1951 bis 1953 in Chicago. Durch das Studium am Illinois Institute of Technology, genauer: am dortigen Illinois Institute of Design, aber auch am Arbeitsplatz beim Bauhaus-Architekten Bertrand Goldberg. Zu den Bekanntschaften in Chicago, einer wahren Fundgrube für Architekten, gehörte auch Frank Lloyd Wright. Ich traf ihn das erste Mal in der Chicago Loop, auf der Straße gehend, mit Hut, Stock und Gehrock, und später in seiner Sommerschule in Spring Green, Wisconsin, das mit einer japanisch anmutenden Landschaft vergleichbar ist.

Auch der Lernprozess des Fotografierens gehörte in diese erste Phase von Begegnungen, und ich begann, mein eigenes Fotoarchiv über Mies van der Rohe und die „Chicago School of Architecture" aufzubauen. Das Dokumentieren und Interpretieren mit der Kamera wurde zu einer lebenslangen Aufgabe. Es begann 1951 in einem Fotografiekurs am Illinois Institute of Design (the late Bauhaus of Moholy Nagy). Die Aufgabe war, ein Fotogramm zu machen. In Aran Suskind, Professor am Illinois Institute of Design, fand ich einen guten Fotolehrmeister, einen der weltbesten. Über ihn konnte ich mit dem letzten Geld eine Rolleicord-Fotokamera kaufen. Meine erste Aufnahme machte ich vom Farnsworth-Haus in Plano, Illinois, von Mies van der Rohe, für die ich vom Museum of Modern Art aus New York eine gute Kritik bekam. Ein Professor der Architektur am Institute of Design, der mich beim Vergrößern dieses Bildes beobachtete, fragte mich, ob ich dieses Sujet aus Japan hatte. Es war für mich der erste Hinweis, wo sich in der Gegenwart fernöstliche Traditionen und westliche Ideen begegneten.

Fotografien von Architektur einen poetischen Rahmen zu verleihen, ist für mich die Kunst all der Wahrheiten, die das Leben erzählt. Das Ablichten in schwarzweiß in allen Helligkeitsstufen ist eine Sichtweise, die das Bildmotiv auf das Wesentliche reduzieren lässt. Mit Fotos Architektur zu entdecken, ist für mich das „Religiöseste", was man tun kann.

Den Einstieg in die fernöstliche Architektur erhielt ich in Chicago vom Geschwisterpaar Chang aus Shanghai: von Pao-Chi, Master of Architecture unter Mies van der Rohe am Illinois Institute of Technology, und ihrem Bruder Chao-Kang, ebenfalls mit Master of Architecture unter Walter Gropius an der Harvard University in Boston. Dies war der Beginn meines Themas „West meets East".

Im Jahre 1955 entstand dann mein erstes Buch „Tempel und Teehaus in Japan". Es war eine Zusammenfassung meiner sechsmonatigen Japanreise zum Thema des klassischen japanischen Pavillonbaus und seiner Bedeutung für die Gegenwart. Japan habe ich dabei mit den Augen von Mies gesehen und ihm ein Exemplar zugestellt. Daraufhin bat er mich um 50 Exemplare für seine Studenten, und er lud mich ein, über sein Werk ein Buch zu machen. Dies entstand in den Sommermonaten 1963 und 1964 in Chicago und erschien unter dem Titel „Mies van der Rohe – die Kunst der Struktur". Für den Titel hielt ich mich an das Essay von Paul Hindemith über J. S. Bach. Dort hieß es, mit der Kunst der Fuge habe Bach das Höchste erreicht. Auch Mies hat dies in seiner Schaffenszeit in Chicago von 1937 bis 1969 getan: mit der Wahrheit der sichtbaren Konstruktion in Stahl und Glas.

Frank Lloyd Wright: pig sty, Taliesin East, Wisconsin, USA, 1950, featuring low-slung roof eaves (photo 1953)
Granite stone building in Valle Verzasca, Ticino, Switzerland, unknown architect (photo 2000)

Frank Lloyd Wright: Schweinestall, Taliesin East, Wisconsin, USA, 1950, Dachformation bis zum Boden (Foto 1953)
Bauform in Granitsteinen im Valle Verzasca, Tessin, Schweiz, anonyme Architektur (Foto 2000)

Conversations with Mies

Encounters with other people also give form to one's own history. For life is a process of encountering. In the case of Mies van der Rohe in Chicago, I encountered an architecture of intellectual content and subsequently felt obligated to pass on this legacy. Mies could be portrayed in the following terms: overtly expressive, reflective, introverted, taciturn, rigorous in his architectural ideas, and very precise in his implementation of them. Elegance and opulence were reflected his heightened feeling for life.

Mies told me that he always focused on structure because it was objective and legible in terms of its development. Every building has to be structured and, in this sense, structure is the primary element of building. For me, architects can be divided into two camps: the curved and the straight, or put another way, the organic cave in contrast to the structured tent. The clarity of structure derives from the coexistence of "compliance" which first makes the tectonic design possible.

Rather than giving lectures in his graduate courses at the Illinois Institute of Technology in Chicago, Mies reviewed students' work at their drawing boards. Students could sit and listen to his critiques and take part in them. He always endeavored to explain architecture using a few, well-chosen words. For him architecture was vigorous, concrete, and straightforward. Modernism was visible, a locus where the technological, cultural, and democratic progress of a society succinctly merged into an elegant commercial and residential world.

I have happy memories of a wonderful dinner with Mies in his apartment on Chicago's Ontario Street – now renamed Mies Van Der Rohe Way. Martinis were served before and after the meal, and the food was complemented by a Mosel wine. After a while, I realized I had drunken a little too much of the delicious wine, so to check if I could still stand up, I rose up out of my chair with my glass in my hand while still talking – falling over in front of Mies was out of the question. My taxi driver subsequently smelt the alcohol on my breath and tried to take me on a detour. However, I saw what he was up to and told him to take me home by the most direct route.

Mies was a father figure and concerned himself with the well-being of those around him. In the summer of 1963, when I went to Chicago while working on a book about him, he waited two days before meeting with me, explaining that he felt I should have time to acclimatize. He was a reserved, almost shy character. I asked whether I could record our conversation on tape. However, as I was about to begin, he excused himself for a moment and I realized that he preferred our conversation not to be recorded. Spontaneous talk was too imprecise for him – thinking was his strength.

In 1952, I worked on a design with Pao-Chi Chang for a single-story timber house. We drew the design perfectly in Indian ink on Strathmore cardboard and presented it to Mies. For a long time, he looked at our work in silence and then asked about a very particular detail. It became clear that he had discovered the weak point of our design in this structural detail. Such was the way Mies explained things using a minimum of words.

Mies told one young architect that his motto was William of Orange's phrase, "To begin without the need of hope; to persevere without the expectation of success." However, he explained, "without hope" did not mean hopeless. This attitude was defiant, like having the knowledge of a path still unknown to others. As a struggle, it was perseverance without success. It referred to the unconditional belief in one's own path – even without acknowledgement. Anyone engaging with the legacy of Mies cannot separate his work and his personality; his work renders his exertion visible, his capacity to concentrate on the essential. The legacy left to us by Mies is therefore to be understood as an ethics of design and building, an endeavor to achieve beauty with radiance from within.

In 1964, my editor from Artemis Verlag in Zurich wanted Mies, himself, to replace me as author of the book on which I was working. At the time I was in Basel and Mies told me over the phone that the editor wanted to meet him in Berlin. However, he told the editor that there would only be a meeting if I, the author was present. Mies's claim to truth, one firmly anchored in his work and ethos, challenges all those who do not live in the truth! The meeting did not take place and I remained the author of the book.

Gespräche mit Mies

Durch Begegnungen mit Menschen verwirklicht sich auch die eigene Geschichte. Denn wirkliches Leben ist Begegnen. Bei Mies van der Rohe in Chicago begegnete ich einer Architektur geistiger Inhalte und fühlte mich verpflichtet, dieses „Erbe" an Architektur zu vermitteln. Mies könnte so porträtiert werden: massiver Ausdruck, nachdenklich, introvertiert, wortkarg, streng in seinen architektonischen Vorstellungen und sehr genau in seinen Ausführungen. Eleganz und Reichtum entsprachen seinem gesteigerten Lebensgefühl.

Mies sagte mir, dass er sich immer an die Konstruktion halte, weil sie objektiv und in ihr eine Entwicklung ablesbar ist. Jedes Bauwerk muss konstruiert werden: Die Konstruktion ist darum das Primäre im Bauen. So sind für mich die Architekten in zwei Lager geteilt: Die Krummen und die Geraden. Oder anders ausgedrückt: die organische Höhle im Gegensatz zum konstruktiven Zelt. Die Klarheit der Konstruktion geht auf das Nebeneinander des „Gehorchens" zurück, welches die tektonische Gestalt erst ermöglicht.

Bei seinen Graduate Courses am Illinois Institute of Technology in Chicago gab Mies keine Vorlesungen. Er kam zu den Studenten an den Zeichentisch. Die Studenten konnten sich bei seinen Kritiken hinsetzen und daran teilnehmen. Er war stets bemüht, mit wenigen klaren Worten die Architektur zu begründen. Bei ihm war Architektur ein Ort der Ausgelassenheit, des Anschaulichen und Überschaubaren. Moderne war für ihn sichtbar, wo technischer, kultureller und demokratischer Fortschritt einer Gesellschaft prägnant in eine elegante Arbeits- und Wohnwelt übergeht.

Gerne erinnere ich mich an ein gutes Chicken-Dinner bei Mies, in seiner Wohnung an der Ontario Street in Chicago – heute die Mies-van-der-Rohe-Allee. Serviert wurde ein Mahl mit Martinis: vor und nach dem Essen. Zur Mahlzeit gab es Mosel-Wein. Mit der Zeit war es doch etwas zu viel Alkohol. Darum stand ich im Gespräch mit dem Glas in der Hand auf, um zu sehen, ob ich noch stehen konnte; vor Mies hinzufallen, wäre für mich unmöglich gewesen. Erst der Taxichauffeur bemerkte meine Alkoholfahne und wollte mich in eine falsche Richtung fahren. Doch ich erkannte sein Vorhaben und bat ihn, mich auf dem direkten Weg nach Hause zu bringen. Mies war eine Vaterfigur und nahm an allem menschlichen Wohlergehen teil: Als ich im Sommer 1963 in Chicago für ein Buchprojekt über ihn eintraf, hat er mich erst nach zwei Tagen empfangen, mit der Begründung, dass ich mich doch zuerst einleben müsse. Er war zurückhaltend, fast scheu. So wollte ich etwa das Gespräch mit ihm auf ein Band aufnehmen. Doch als ich beginnen wollte, musste er auf die Toilette, und ich wusste, dass er keine Tonaufnahme wollte. Das spontane Sprechen war ihm zu unpräzis: Denken war seine Stärke.

Im Jahre 1952 erstellte ich zusammen mit Pao-Chi Chang ein Projekt für ein einstöckiges Holzhaus. Das Haus wurde perfekt in Tusch auf Strathmore-Karton gezeichnet, welches wir dann Mies vorlegten. Er sah unser Werk eine lange Zeit stumm an und fragte dann nach einem ganz speziellen Detail. In der Tat hatte er unseren Schwachpunkt nur an diesem Konstruktionsdetail entdeckt. Es war seine Art, Dinge ohne viele Worte zu erklären.

Zu einem jungen Architekten sagte Mies, sein Motto sei das Wort von Wilhelm von Oranien: „Ohne Hoffnung anfangen, ohne Erfolg weitermachen." Ohne Hoffnung bedeute jedoch nicht hoffnungslos. Diese Haltung sei wie Trotz oder wie ein Wissen um den Weg, den noch kein anderer kenne. Als Kampf sei es ein Weitermachen ohne Erfolg. Es bedeute den unbedingten Glauben an den eigenen Weg – auch ohne Applaus. Wer sich mit dem Erbe von Mies befasst, kann Werk und Persönlichkeit nicht trennen, lässt doch sein Werk sein Bemühen sichtbar werden, sich selbst auf das Wesentliche zu konzentrieren. Das Erbe, das uns Mies hinterlassen hat, ist deshalb als eine Ethik des Gestaltens und Bauens zu verstehen, ein Bemühen um das Schöne mit dem Glanz von innen.

Im Jahre 1964 wollte mein Verleger vom Artemis Verlag in Zürich Mies selbst als Autor meines Buches erzwingen. Damals war ich in Basel, und Mies teilte mir telefonisch mit, dass der Verleger ihn in Berlin treffen wollte. Doch er sagte ihm, ein Treffen käme nur zustande, wenn auch der Autor Werner Blaser anwesend wäre. Der Wahrheitsanspruch von Mies, der fest in der Gesinnung und Werk verankert ist, fordert all diejenigen zum Widerspruch auf, die nicht in der Wahrheit leben! So kam diese Begegnung nicht zustande, und ich blieb der Autor dieses Buches.

Georges Chedanne: Le Parisien newspaper offices, Paris, 1904–1906 (photo 1973)
Mies van der Rohe: Chicago Federal Center, USA, 1959–1964 (photo 1973)

Georges Chedanne: Zeitungshaus „Le Parisien" Paris, 1904–1906 (Foto 1973)
Mies van der Rohe: Chicago Federal Center, USA 1959–1964 (Foto 1973)

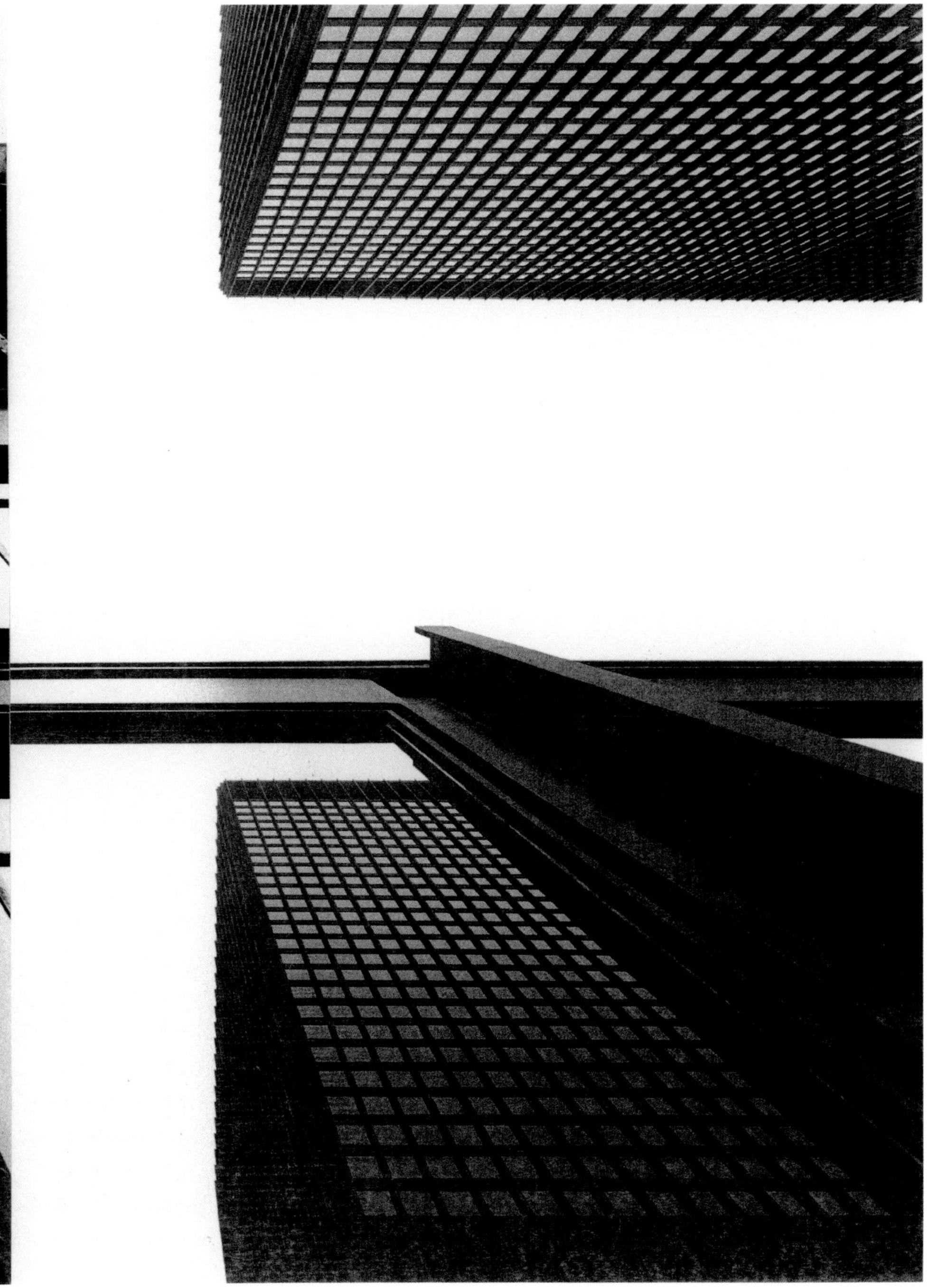

Succeeding Mies

Mies initially wanted the landscape architect and IIT lecturer Alfred Caldwell (1903–1996) to succeed him as head of the IIT Architecture Department. Both as a designer and teacher, Caldwell was a suitable successor. He saw proportionality and rhythm as integral elements and expressions of morphology. The volume of a building in itself showed him the extent to which ideas were based on originality and formed an optimal synthesis of function and form. In his eyes, human being, nature, and architecture formed a unified whole. However, in the end Mies decided to pass his position to a member of the younger generation: George Danforth, who had studied under Mies and worked in his architectural office. He was one of the figures at IIT who enabled the Mies School to continue to flourish.

Another intelligent and congenial member of Mies's office was the engineer and architect Myron Goldsmith, who was something of a philosopher. As "architect in charge" he was integrally involved in building the Farnsworth House. He was referred to as a "poet of structure." In the period "after Mies," Goldsmith was regarded as one of IIT's most successful teachers.

Someone whom Mies held in particularly high esteem was the architect Phyllis Lambert from Montreal, who completed her Master's degree in Architecture under Mies's supervision in 1962. While I was a guest in her patrician house in Montreal, I opened a window to get some fresh air and in the process triggered an alarm installed to protect her extensive art collection. She also had an apartment in Chicago on the twenty-sixth floor in the tower block designed by Mies on Lake Shore Drive on Lake Michigan, where she invited Mies and me to dinner. After eating, she ordered her guests to sit in silence so that everyone could fully experience the sunset over the wide expanse of lake.

Following Mies's death, the two foremost experts on his work, Phyllis Lambert, who had a family connection to the Seagram Building in New York, and the Chicago-based architect Dirk Lohan, Mies's grandson, both embraced postmodernism. The architect Gene Summers, who was Mies's right-hand man in his office from 1950 to 1966, also later took his playful artistry in a postmodernist direction. This left me as one of the few architects who continued to develop Mies's architectural principles and to make them my own. I think it is a pity that in the period "after Mies" there were not more of us who continued to maintain and develop his approach.

Together with Werner Sobek, the talented German-American architect, Helmut Jahn formulated the term "archi-engineering" for a book he was working on in collaboration with me. This concept, which can also be seen as informed by the spirit of Mies, entails an amalgamation of architecture and engineering with the goal of developing a high-tech architecture out of structural details. "Archi-engineering" involves a constructive process of planning and design and is based on the collective work of architects, engineers, and building services engineers.

Nachfolge Mies

Als Nachfolger für die Leitung der Architekturabteilung am IIT wollte Mies zuerst den Landschaftsarchitekten und Lehrer am IIT Alfred Caldwell (1903–1996) verpflichten. Planerische und pädagogische Eignung waren bei ihm gleichermaßen adäquat. Für ihn waren Maßstäblichkeit und Rhythmisierung integrale Elemente und Bilder des Gestalthaften. Allein die Fülle eines Bauwerks zeigte ihm, wie sehr Ideen auf Originalität fußen und eine optimale Synthese aus Funktion und Gestalt bilden. Mensch–Natur–Architektur war ihm eine Ganzheit. Mies entschied sich jedoch, die Nachfolge einer jüngeren Generation zu übertragen: George Danforth, einem Schüler und Mitarbeiter seines Büros. Er war am IIT eine Persönlichkeit, der die Schule Mies weiterleben ließ.

Ein weiterer intelligenter und sympathischer Mitarbeiter war der Ingenieur und Architekt Myron Goldsmith, ein Philosoph im Büro Mies. Als „architect in charge“ hat er das Farnsworth-Haus mitgeprägt. Man nannte ihn „poet of structure“. „After Mies“ wirkte er am IIT als einer der erfolgreichsten Pädagogen.

Eine der bedeutendsten Frauen, die Mies schätzte, ist die Architektin Phyllis Lambert von Montreal. Ihren Master of Architecture machte sie 1962 noch unter Mies. In ihrem Patrizierhaus in Montreal, wo ich als Gast weilte, öffnete ich das Fenster um frische Luft einzuatmen, nicht wissend, dass ich dabei wegen ihrer großen Kunstsammlung einen Großalarm auslöste. Ihre zweite Wohnung war in Chicago, zuoberst im Wohnturm von Mies, im Lake Shore Drive, am Michigansee, im 26. Stockwerk. Sie lud mich zusammen mit Mies zum Dinner ein. Nach dem Essen ordnete sie eine stille Zeit an, damit alle zusammen in Stille den Sonnenuntergang auf der weiten Fläche des Sees innerlich erleben konnten.

Die beiden großen Mies-Kenner, Phyllis Lambert, familiär verbunden mit dem Seagram-Office-Gebäude in New York, und der in Chicago praktizierende Architekt Dirk Lohan, ein Enkel von Mies, bekannten sich nach dem Tod von Mies zur Postmoderne. Auch der Architekt Gene Summers, die rechte Hand in Mies' Büro von 1950 bis 1966, wandte seine spielerischen Kunstfertigkeiten später der Postmoderne zu. So war ich einer der wenigen, der die Architekturprinzipien von Mies weiter entwickelte und zu meinen eigenen machte. Schade, dass das „After Mies“ so wenig konkrete Gefolgschaft fand.

Der talentierte deutsch-amerikanische Architekt Helmut Jahn schuf zusammen mit Werner Sobek und für ein Buch mit mir den Begriff „Archi-Engineering“, der, wohl auch im Geist Mies', auf ein Zusammenführen von Architektur- und Ingenieurskunst setzt, mit dem Ziel, die Gestalt aus dem Detail zur Hightech-Architektur zu entwickeln. Dieses „Archi-Engineering“ ist ein aufbauendes Planen und Gestalten, es lebt von der gemeinsamen Entwicklungsarbeit von Architekten, Ingenieuren und Gebäudetechnikern.

Mies van der Rohe: National Gallery, Berlin, steel support, 1962–1968 (photo 2010)
Katsura Imperial Villa, Kyoto, 1602: Shokin-tei tea pavilion (photo 1953)

Mies van der Rohe: Nationalgalerie Berlin, Stahl-Stütze, 1962–1968 (Foto 2010)
Kaiserliche Katsura-Villa in Kyoto, 1602: Teepavillon Shokin-tei (Foto 1953)

Kyoto with Zen – an Architecture of Stillness

Already during my trade apprenticeship in Basel I had read Tetsura Yoshida's acclaimed book *The Japanese House.* I took the publication with me during my sixth-month trip to Japan, during which time I stayed in the temple city of Kyoto. The classical temple and teahouse in everyday architecture in Japan exhibit a perfection that has retained its esteem over centuries. The pavilions give rise to an ambivalent feeling that vacillates between admiration of an aesthetic spatial sequence and wonder at the expression of emptiness, which has also influenced our modernism.

During my six-month sojourn in 1953, I stayed in Kyoto's Sakyo-ku district in a Japanese building modeled on the Katsura Imperial Villa. I lived like those around me. People understood my English and I could speak a little Japanese. I spent my days visiting temples and teahouses, and travelling by public transport. The fact that I knew what I wanted helped me to find my intended destinations without much knowledge of Japanese and without having to resort to hailing taxis. This success born of sheer determination later proved a minor sensation among my friends in Basel.

After the period of seeing and learning in Chicago, my experience in Japan in 1953 was more one of discovery and application. In this process, I was helped by a number of thinkers and scholars in Kyoto, above all M. Miura, professor and head of the psychiatric faculty at Kyoto University, and his assistants. It was they who introduced me to Japanese Zen Buddhism. As a gift to them, I gave them signed copies of books by the philosopher Karl Jaspers, who lived in Basel.

Other significant encounters included those with the Zen Buddhist abbot Kobori Sohaku and the abbess Ruth Fuller-Sasaki, both from the Daitoku-ji temple district in Kyoto. Ruth Fuller later visited me in Basel, where her sightseeing consisted of travelling to and fro across the Rhine on the (motorless) Münster Ferry, thus exhibiting one of her inner Zen qualities! Thanks to these acquaintances, I developed a deep understanding of Japanese architecture and clarity about what simplicity in Zen expresses. I recognized parallels between the architectural principles of Mies and Japanese design. This gave rise to a need to document the past and translate it into the present, and thereby the incentive to create books on Japanese architecture.

Years later, while I was on a trip to Japan I had organized for friends from Switzerland, we met up with the writer Adolf Muschg. In accordance with Japanese custom, he and his wife, Atsuko Kanto-Muschg, as our hosts, invited us to a traditional meal in a temple pavilion in Kyoto. In 1953, during my stay in Kyoto, Atsuko was still a little girl and living in the same building in Sakyo-ku as I did, where she marveled at her tall, blonde European neighbor.

The ideal at the heart of the Japanese "architecture of stillness" is to be found in the building ethos, in the intellectual stance from which the work gains its design strength. This is particularly evident in the classical temple and residential buildings in Kyoto. As representations, they show us a largely lost congruence between living and residing: the human being in space, meditative sitting, the inclusion of the exterior space, the actuality of tradition and the close, respectful relationship to nature. This Japanese spirit is not something we can or should seek to realize in our "Western" architecture. However, given that the development of our modern architecture has so obviously been influenced by Japanese concepts, it is worthwhile exploring Japan's classical buildings in detail as a source of design ideas that can help us create our own "architecture of stillness."

The internally fixed place to which one belongs has been my constant companion during my working life. This self-awareness provided a foundation for my development. I discovered the essential elements of classical Japanese architecture and realized that it was possible to forge a continuity that would bring it into the present. As parallels to the classical temple and residential buildings of old Japan, Mies's "skin and skeleton" concepts strengthened my own view of the world, my endeavor to understand history as present, and my orientation towards an architecture that repeatedly finds new expression between the assertion of tried and tested values and the openness of the prevailing spirit of the time. Historical reference points generate curiosity.

Kyoto mit Zen – eine Baukunst der Stille

Schon als Handwerkslehrling in Basel habe ich das wichtige Buch „Das japanische Wohnhaus" von Tetsura Yoshida erworben. Es war der Begleiter auf meiner halbjährigen Japanreise in der Tempelstadt Kyoto. In der Tat zeigt das klassische Tempel- und Teehaus in der Alltagsarchitektur eine Vollkommenheit, welche über Jahrhunderte aktuell geblieben ist. Diese Pavillons erzeugen ein ambivalentes Gefühl, das sich zwischen der Bewunderung für eine ästhetische Raumfolge und dem Staunen über den unglaublichen Ausdruck der Leere bewegt, der auch unsere Moderne tangiert.

Bei meinem halbjährigen Aufenthalt 1953 lebte ich im Quartier Sakyo-ku in Kyoto in einem japanischen Haus nach dem Vorbild der kaiserlichen Katsura-Villa und pflegte dort die heimische Tradition. Man verstand mein Englisch und ich ein wenig das Japanische. Täglich besuchte ich die Tempel- und Teehausbauten – alles mit öffentlichen Verkehrsmitteln und örtlicher Sprache. Ich wusste, was ich wollte, darum kam ich immer auch ohne große japanische Sprachkenntnisse und ohne Taxi an den richtigen Ort. Mein zielbewusstes Streben wurde im Nachhinein von meinen Basler Freunden wie eine kleine Sensation wahrgenommen.

Nach dem Sehen und Lernen in Chicago bedeutete Japan im Jahre 1953 für mich eher ein Erkennen und Verwerten. Dabei halfen mir eine Zahl von Denkern und Wissenschaftlern in Kyoto, allen voran M. Miura, Professor und Vorsteher an der psychiatrischen Fakultät, und seine Assistenten. Sie führten mich in den Geist des japanischen Zen-Buddhismus ein. Mitgebracht hatte ich ihnen signierte Bücher des in Basel lebenden Philosophen Karl Jaspers.

Dazu kamen die Begegnungen mit dem zen-buddhistischen Abt Kobori Sohaku und der Äbtin Ruth Fuller-Sasaki, beide vom Daitôku-ji Tempelbezirk in Kyoto. Später besuchte mich Ruth Fuller in Basel. Ihr Sightseeing bestand nur aus einer Stunde Hin-und-Her-Fahren über den Rhein mit der Münsterfähre (ohne Motor) – eine ihrer inneren Zen-Eigenschaften! Dank dieser Bekanntschaften entwickelte sich bei mir ein tiefes Verständnis für die japanische Architektur, eine Klarheit darüber, was Einfachheit im Zen aussagt. Ich erkannte Parallelen zwischen den architektonischen Prinzipien von Mies und Japan. Daraus entstanden mein Bedürfnis, das Vergangene zu dokumentieren und ins Gegenwärtige zu übertragen, und in der Folge davon meine Japanbücher.

Auf einer Japanreise, die ich Jahrzehnte später für gute Freunde aus der Schweiz organisierte, war auch der Schriftsteller Adolf Muschg gegenwärtig. Er hat uns als Gastgeber zusammen mit seiner Frau Atsuko Kanto-Muschg nach japanischer Sitte in einem Tempelpavillon in Kyoto zu einem traditionellen Mahl eingeladen. Im Jahr 1953, während meines Aufenthalts in Kyoto, war Muschgs Frau Atsuko im Haus in Sakyô-ku, wo ich wohnte, noch ein kleines Mädchen und hat mich als großen blonden Europäer bewundert!

Das Vorbildliche in der japanischen „Architektur der Stille" ist in der Baugesinnung zu suchen, im Geistigen, aus welchem das Werk seine Gestalt gewinnt. Am Beispiel der klassischen Tempel- und Wohnbauten in Kyoto wird dies in besonderer Weise deutlich. Diese Darstellungen zeigen uns die weitgehend verlorengegangene Übereinstimmung von Leben und Wohnen: den Menschen im Raum, sein meditatives Sitzen, die Einbeziehung des Außenraums, die Gegenwärtigkeit der Tradition und die enge, ehrfurchtsvolle Beziehung zur Natur. Es kann zwar nicht japanischer Geist sein, den wir in unserem „westlichen" Bauen zu verwirklichen haben. Da sich aber unsere moderne Architektur in so offensichtlicher Nähe zur alt-japanischen entwickelt hat, lohnt es sich, am Beispiel der klassischen Bauwerke Japans unsere eigene Entwurfsarbeit bis ins Letzte zu schulen, damit auch unsere Architektur eine Baukunst der Stille werden kann.

Der innerlich feste Ort, zu welchem man gehört, war der ständige Begleiter meines Arbeitslebens. Auf diesem Selbstbewusstsein konnte ich meine Entwicklung aufbauen. Ich entdeckte das Wesentliche der alt-japanischen Architektur und sah, dass diese Tradition mit Kontinuität ins Heute zu bringen war. Der „Skin and Skeleton"-Gedanke von Mies stärkte als Parallele zu den klassischen Tempel- und Wohnbauten Alt-Japans mein eigenes Weltbild, das Bemühen, die Geschichte als Gegenwart zu verstehen, die Orientierung an einer Baukunst, die sich zwischen Behauptung der alten bewährten Werte und der Offenheit für den jeweiligen Geist der Zeit immer wieder neu zum Ausdruck bringt. Historische Bezugspunkte machen neugierig!

Mies van der Rohe: Farnsworth House porch, Plano, Illinois, USA, 1945–1950 (photo 1953)
Shugaku-in Imperial Villa, Kyoto, Japan, 1629 (photo 1980)

Mies van der Rohe: Porch im Farnsworth House, Plano, Ilinois, USA, 1945–1950 (Foto 1953)
Kaiserliche Sommervilla Shugaku-in, Kyoto, Japan, 1629 (Foto 1980)

Basel as a City of Architecture

Architects are constantly on the move; for them the journey is a response to a kind of yearning. Journeys with concrete objectives therefore acquire a very different status. Being settled in another place means the drive to travel has a point of departure; travelling to a place means transforming it into an educational objective. For me, travelling also means "being on the way to myself."

Being on the road led me into a new world that lent more precise contours to images in my mind, whose effect has unfolded throughout my life. Travelling is guided by curiosity and the interest in acquiring knowledge; it stimulates ideas and ideals and fuses past times with the present. I aim for places of yearning and celebrate what I see like an initiation. Yet, in the *Tao Te Ching* by Lao Tzu it is written, "Without leaving my house, I know the world."

After six years abroad, I returned to Basel with a comprehensive and interesting collection of photos of buildings by Mies in Chicago and pavilion architecture in Japan. My wealth of experience also enabled me to establish myself as a well-regarded furniture designer. I used everything I had documented and learned since 1955 to create my own design office – initially in Neuweilerstrasse and later in St. Alban-Vorstadt. The path leading from Mies, via Japan, to my own design work became a concrete reality. I created furniture from within myself, unaffected by prevailing fashion trends. In response to my designs, Georg Schmidt, the then director of the Kunstmuseum Basel, remarked that he was not sure whether my furniture was twenty years behind or twenty years ahead of its time.

My experimental field is now one that covers several decades. It includes pieces of furniture that unfortunately never reached the manufacturing stage. None of them were the result of spur-of-the-moment ideas; my experimentation has always been based on systematic design that exhibits clarity down to the last detail and does justice to the materials employed. Approaching design in this way, in turn, led to other thematic focuses, such as "structure as aesthetic" and the "art of joint."

In order to promote Basel as a city of architecture, I founded the "Basel Architecture Lectures" in 1980 and continued to organize them until 2003. Thanks to the participation of contemporary master architects in this lecture series, they generated a broad discussion about architecture in Basel. Speakers created a vivid architectural dialog for the younger generation. Addressing themes such as "versatile building" – which was repeatedly discussed – they influenced and activated our senses. Ultimately, what constitutes good building is culture and addressing it effectively requires structured, interdisciplinary collaboration between all those involved in the construction process. As a means of promoting such collaboration, the 200 lectures and architectural visions making up the lectures series for the most part contributed to the emergence of a meaningful, internationally relevant building culture in Basel.

The future cannot be predicted; there is no such thing as precise prophecy. However, the prognosis that the world is going to have to deal with all sorts of environmental problems is undoubtedly correct. Crucial in this context is the concept of awareness. We must become aware of this challenge and constantly extend the knowledge required to master it. The hopes of seven billion people are founded on this awareness: Can the world's intractable environmental problems perhaps be solved after all, or is this merely wishful thinking?

Basel als Architektur-Stadt

Architekten, zu denen auch ich gehöre, sind immer unterwegs, denn für sie geht es beim Reisen um Sehnsuchtsorte. Reisen mit Zielvorstellungen bekommen deshalb einen ganz anderen Stellenwert. Sesshaftigkeit an einem anderen Ort bedeutet, dem Reisetrieb einen Ausgangspunkt zu geben, Reisen an einen Ort, diesen in ein Lernziel zu verwandeln. Reisen heißt für mich immer auch, „auf dem Weg zu sich sein".

Das Unterwegssein führte mich in eine neue Welt, in der Traumbilder aufgefrischt wurden, welche ihre Wirkung in meinem Leben entfalteten. Das Reisen folgt der Neugier und dem Erkenntnisinteresse, es lässt Ideen und Ideale entstehen und verschmilzt vergangene Zeiten mit der Gegenwart. Ich strebe Sehnsuchtsorte an und feiere das Gesehene wie eine Initiation. Und doch heißt es bei Laotse im Buch „Tao te king": „Nicht zum Tore hinausgehen und die Welt erkennen."

Nach sechsjährigem Auslandaufenthalt wieder in Basel, hatte ich eine sehenswerte und vollständige Fotosammlung der Bauwerke von Mies in Chicago und der Pavillon-Architektur in Japan. Aber auch mein kreatives Schaffen im Möbelbau wurde hoch geschätzt. Ich transponierte das vielseitig Dokumentierte und Gelernte seit 1955 im eigenen Büro – zuerst an der Neuweilerstraße und später in der St. Alban-Vorstadt. Der Weg von Mies über Japan zum Ich wurde Wirklichkeit. Es entstanden von innen heraus eigene Möbelkreationen, jenseits aller modischen Strömungen. Dies veranlasste Georg Schmidt, den damaligen Direktor des Kunstmuseums in Basel, zu folgender Aussage: Er wisse nicht, ob mein Möbeldesign 20 Jahre zurück oder 20 Jahre voraus sei.

Mein Experimentierfeld hat sich inzwischen über mehrere Jahrzehnte gehalten. Es entstanden Möbel, die leider jedoch keine Produktionsstufe erreichten. Nie waren sie Alltagseinfälle, sondern immer einem konsequenten, materialgerechten und bis ins Detail klaren Gestalten verpflichtet. Daraus ergaben sich weitere Arbeitsthemen wie „Statik als Ästhetik" oder „Kunst der Fuge".

Um Basel als Architektur-Stadt zu fördern, schuf ich 1980 die „Basler Architektur-Vorträge", die ich bis 2003 organisierte. Dank der Teilnahme von aktuellen Meisterarchitekten entfalteten sie eine positive Auswirkung auf das Architekturgeschehen in unserer Stadt, ließen sie in Basel eine breite Diskussion über Architektur entstehen. Die Vortragenden schufen für die junge Generation eine bildwirksame Architektursprache. Mit Themen wie „wandlungsfähiges Bauen", welches immer wieder behandelt wurde, beeinflussten und aktivierten sie unsere Sinne. Letztlich ist die Diskussion um gutes Bauen eine kulturelle Frage, die eine strukturierte interdisziplinäre Zusammenarbeit aller Bauschaffenden voraussetzt. In einer Vielzahl von 200 Vorträgen und Visionen ist so in Basel ein breites Verständnis für sinnstiftende Baukultur entstanden.

Man kann die Zukunft nicht voraussagen; exakte Prophezeiungen gibt es nicht. Dennoch ist die Prognose bestimmt richtig, dass die Welt an Umweltproblemen aller Art schwer tragen wird. Wichtig ist in diesem Zusammenhang das Wort „bewusst": Wir müssen uns dieser Herausforderung bewusst werden, müssen unser Wissen über deren Bewältigung stetig erweitern. Im Bewusstwerden liegen die Wahrheit und die Zuversicht von sieben Milliarden Menschen begründet: Können die unlösbaren Umweltprobleme vielleicht doch gelöst werden? Oder bleibt dies nur ein Wunschdenken?

Experiencing Historical Buildings

The cavern is solid, the tent structural. These are oppositions that are supposed to endure one another. However, when the structural no longer radiates through the solid as an architectural truth, the hunt for the pure sculptural form becomes questionable for those who have been trained in objective architecture. In open space we need to use our freedom of movement in the way recommended by Thomas Aquinas: Live in a state of wandering. Life as passing by, passing through, not as duration.

For this reason the local, vernacular buildings explored in my books, such as *The Swiss Farmhouse, The Rock is my Home, Wooden Bridges in Switzerland,* and *Fantasy in Wood*, have a special status for me. The Walser people originally came from the nearby Wallis in Switzerland. The alpine huts in their Alpine settlements in Alagna, which consist of double-story log granaries, are located behind Monte Rosa in Italy. There is a tension between the objective building structure and the subjective design. In the skeletal principle, a clear distinction is made between the structure as fabric and the texture as effect. The horizontal structure created by the enclosed terraces used for hanging and drying harvested produce is characteristic of rural buildings, or Stadel (Scheune), in the Walser region.

In the nineteenth century, two similar styles developed on both sides of the Atlantic: the Ville d'Hiver in Arcachon in France, and the American Victorian style in Galveston, Texas. The row houses in the American town of Galveston on the Atlantic Ocean built around 1900 feature spacious wooden verandahs. Their structural logic links them with the Belle Époque villas of the Ville d'hiver in Arcachon, with France giving them a transatlantic identity.

Even prior to the nineteenth century, fully glazed wooden balconies became a feature of buildings in central La Coruña on the Atlantic in northern Spain. These structural elements are a meter deep and serve as compensation chambers that protect the interior living spaces from the weather. In winter they allow sunlight into the building, while in summer the interiors remain cool. These protective facades on the Casas de las Galerías create a continuous cityscape.

The natural and the earthbound facilitate an understanding of what building can mean. The fundamental character of a material and its utilization are revealed, for example, when stone is laid on stone. On the island of Inisheer in Ireland, enclosures for animals are formed by low stonewalls constructed without mortar. There are no gates and access is only possible by removing and replacing stones. Here, a virtue has been made of the elemental bond to a material.

My journey to Eastern Europe was facilitated by my architectural colleagues, professors Johannes Spalt and Friedrich Kurrent from Vienna. Another colleague associated with the University of Applied Arts in Vienna, the architect Aneta Kamenowa, drew my attention to Bulgarian Renaissance architecture in the mountain village of Koprivistiza. It has become ever more necessary for me to explore local building cultures, and in this respect Eastern Europe offers a great deal.

In the Maramures in the north of Romania, one finds an intact local culture featuring tectonic timber architecture, one that includes wooden Orthodox churches dating back to the seventeenth and eighteenth centuries and log farmhouses surrounded by woven fences and decorated gates. Folklorist and farmhouse researcher Francisc Nistor accompanied me to this remote area. I was interested in learning about the structural problems presented by local building materials and in exploring new ideas from local solutions.

The architect Bernardo Vittone from Turin had a formative influence on the Baroque in Piedmont. His domed churches richly ornamented with stucco are marvels of directed lighting and the organically structured arrangement of rib and shell vaults. Vittone took the ideas developed by the Turin architect Guarini and applied them in small towns surrounding Turin, creating a pragmatic Baroque architecture featuring structural components that also provide integrated decoration.

Siphnos, an island in the Cyclades in Greece, has thus far been spared the negative effects of tourism. Its landscape is shaped by an archaic architecture featuring myriad terraces and walls. The whitewashed, natural stone masonry

Erleben von Baudenkmälern

Massiv ist die Höhle, konstruktiv das Zelt. Es sind Gegensätze, die sich ertragen sollten. Wenn aber das Konstruktive durch das Massive nicht mehr als architektonische Wahrheit ausstrahlt, wird denen, die an der objektiven Baukunst geschult sind, die Jagd nach dem nur plastisch Geformten fragwürdig. Im offenen Raum ist die Bewegungsfreiheit so, wie es Thomas von Aquin formulierte: Im Zustand des Wanderns leben. Leben als Vorübergehen, Durchgehen, nicht als Dauer.

Aus diesem Grund haben die heimische Bauten in meinen Büchern wie „Bauernhaus der Schweiz", „Der Fels ist mein Haus", „Gedeckte Holzbrücken und „Fantasie in Holz" für mich einen ganz besonderen Stellenwert. Ursprünglich kamen die Walser aus dem benachbarten Wallis (Schweiz). Die Alphütten ihrer Bergkolonien in Alagna befinden sich hinter dem Monte Rosa in Italien. Sie bestehen aus zweistöckigen Blockspeichern. Die objektive Baustruktur steht in Spannung zur subjektiven Gestalt. Im Skelettprinzip wird klar unterschieden zwischen der Struktur als Gefüge und der Textur als Wirkung. Die von mehreren Seiten umschlossenen Terrassen zum Trocknen und Aufhängen von Erntegut prägen mit der horizontalen Gliederung den Baustil der Walser Stadel.

Diesseits und jenseits des Atlantiks entstanden im 19. Jahrhundert zwei ähnliche Baustile: in Arcachon mit der Ville d'hiver in Frankreich und in Galveston (Texas) im American Victorian Style. Die Reihenhäuser der amerikanischen Kleinstadt Galveston am atlantischen Ozean bestehen aus großräumigen Terrassen in Holzkonstruktion, gebaut um 1900. Durch ihre konstruktive Logik sind sie mit den Villen der Belle Époque der Ville d'hiver im französischen Arcachon auf der Gegenseite des Atlantiks verbunden – eine transatlantische Gleichheit!

Noch vor dem 19. Jahrhundert entstanden die Holzvorbauten im innerstädtischen La Coruña (am Atlantik in Nordspanien). Diese vollverglasten Bauelemente von einem Meter Tiefe dienen als Ausgleichskammern, welche die Wohnräume vor dem Wetter schützen: Im Winter gelangt ohne Abkühlung viel Sonnenlicht in die Gebäude; im Sommer bleibt es im Innern kühl. Diese funktionsfähigen Wetterschutzfassaden der „Casas de las Galerías" prägen ein kontinuierliches Stadtbild.

Das Natürliche und Erdgebundene ermöglicht ein Verständnis von dem, was Bauen bedeuten kann. Ein Material und seine Verwendung werden in seinen elementaren Grundlagen gezeigt, etwa wenn Stein auf Stein gelegt wird. Mörtellos aufeinander geschichtete, niedrige Steinwälle bilden auf der Insel Inisheer in Irland das Gehege für Haustiere. Zum Betreten werden Steine abgebaut und dann wieder aufgebaut. Es gibt kein Tor. Aus der elementaren Gebundenheit an ein Material ist hier eine Tugend geworden.

Der Weg nach Osteuropa wurde mir auch von den Architektenkollegen, den Professoren Johannes Spalt und Friedrich Kurrent, von Wien aus eröffnet. Ebenfalls aus dem Kreise der Hochschule für Angewandte Kunst in Wien hat mich die Architektin Aneta Kamenowa zur bulgarischen Renaissance-Architektur in das Bergdorf Koprivistiza geführt. Osteuropa liefert einen wichtigen Beitrag für die nötig gewordene Besinnung auf das heimische Bauen.

In der Region Maramures im Norden von Rumänien trifft man noch auf eine intakte Kultur der Bewohner und auf ihre tektonische Holzarchitektur. Die heute erhaltenen orthodoxen Holzkirchen des 17. und 18. Jahrhunderts und die Bauernhäuser im Blockbau, welche von geflochtenen Zäunen und geschmückten Toren umrahmt sind, zeugen davon. Der Volkskundler und Bauernhausforscher Francisc Nistor begleitete mich in diese abgelegene Gegend. Es ging mir darum, die konstruktiven Probleme heimischer Bausubstanz kennen zu lernen, zu durchdenken und mit neuen Impulsen für uns zurückzukehren.

Der Baumeister Bernardo Vittone in Turin prägte den Barock im Piemont. Die mit Stuck verzierten, kuppelgewölbten Hallenkirchen sind Wunderwerke der Lichtführung und der organisch konstruktiven Gestaltung von Rippen und Haut. Die Experimente des Turiners Guarini wurden vom Piemonteser Architekten Vittone in Kleinstädten in der Gegend um Turin in eine volksnahe, bäuerliche Barockarchitektur umgesetzt. Es entstanden Bauglieder mit konstruktiver Funktion und flächenverbundener Dekoration zugleich.

Siphnos, eine Insel der Kykladen ohne Flughafen, ist vom Tourismus noch verschont. Eine archaische Architektur mit

of the houses lends them a basic, cubic appearance. In the still intact village of Kato Petali, the unembellished block forms of the buildings incorporate primary cubic, conical, and cylindrical forms while still retaining a secure structure. Another fundamental element unifying the architecture of the buildings is the marking of the pathways leading to each house, which have to be renewed every spring.

The city center of Tomsk in Siberia is largely comprised of double- and triple-story buildings built from timber logs. There are two basic typologies of log buildings: only log, and log walls clad with boards. The joins between the logs lend the buildings an elemental, almost archaic character. The log structure is the primary, essential structure, the boards the overlay cladding. The decorative woodwork on the roof crowns and window frames recalls the lace cloths that are hung around icons. It would be hard to find a more original example of an archaic formal motif than those on display in this extremely remote region of Siberia, where the striking appearance of the building facades with their rhythm of window ornamentation is the essence of the local architecture.

My four trips to China brought another necessary dimension to my knowledge of the Far East. During my first trip, which I took in 1972 with my wife Helen at the invitation of the Architecture Society of China, I was able select the places I wished to visit. At the time I was researching the pavilion architecture of the Ming and Qing dynasties. These buildings feature a rationally structured skeleton and organically curved roofs that give expression to the imaginative power that has produced them. Traditional China could be a source of new impetus for the Occident in terms of the perception of architecture and the development of its principles.

The palaces in the royal cities of Rajasthan in northern India present transparency in stone. For me, the goal remained constant: to learn from these marble buildings and to apply the insights I acquired to modern architecture. There is a saying that states, “Building for the future – coming across the past.” These palaces are an illustration of reaching beyond the aesthetic in a quest for the spiritual. Persian domed buildings have always interested me. Isfahan with its beautiful gardens, bridges, mosques, and palaces presents an image that mirrors both the cosmos and paradise. The Islamic, geometrically laid out garden reshapes nature as an artwork. All good architecture aspires to create a world in which the building is a unique structure imbued with atmosphere. In the Rajasthan region of northern India, the palaces are built of white marble, which is used to create wall openings that allow light to permeate and create an almost cosmic effect. Endless spatial transitions and perforations create a masterful play of transparency, as seen in the palace complex of Fatepur Sikri near Agra. This transparency generates lines of sight, makes the concealed accessible, and encourages curiosity in the beholder.

unzähligen Terrassen und Mauern prägt das Landschafts-Bild. Das weiss geschlämmte Bruchsteinmauerwerk der Wohnhäuser bildet eine einfache kubische Erscheinung. Im noch intakten Dorf Kato Petali sind an den schmucklosen Quaderformen der Häuser die elementaren Formen von Kubus, Kegel und Zylinder erhalten und schaffen noch immer eine verlässliche Struktur. Ein weiteres wesentliches Element, welches die Architektur der Häuser zu einem Ganzen verbindet, sind die Bodenmarkierungen der Wege, die zu jedem Haus führen und jedes Frühjahr neu erstellt werden.

Die Innenstadt im sibirischen Tomsk besteht weitgehend aus zwei- bis dreistöckigen Holzblockbauten. Es sind grundsätzlich zwei Typen von Blockbauten: reiner Block oder mit Brettern verschalte Blockwände. Der Strick, wie man diese Verbindung im Blockbau nennt, gibt den Bauten einen elementarischen, beinahe archaischen Charakter. Der Block ist das Elementare, die Verschalung das Verkleidende. Das dekorative Holzwerk des Dachkranzes und der Fensterumrahmungen erinnert an die Spitzentücher, welche um die Ikonen gehängt werden. Es gibt kaum ein ursprünglicheres Beispiel eines archaischen Formmotivs als in dieser weit abgelegenen Region Sibiriens. Die glanzvolle Inszenierung der Hausfassaden mit dem rhythmisierenden Fensterschmuck ist dort das eigentliche Wesen der Baukunst.

Während vier Chinareisen wurden meine Kenntnisse über den Fernen Osten abgerundet. Bei der ersten Reise 1972, zusammen mit meiner Frau Helen und auf Einladung der chinesischen Architekturgesellschaft, durfte ich meine Reiseziele selbst bestimmen. Damals ging es mir darum, über die Pavillon-Architektur der Ming- und Qing-Dynastie zu recherchieren. Das Skelett dieser Bauten ist rational strukturiert; zugleich kommt im organisch geschwungenen Dach die Einbildungskraft zum Ausdruck. Das Abendland könnte vom traditionellen China neue Impulse für das Wahrnehmen von Architektur und für das Herausbilden ihrer Prinzipien empfangen.

Transparenz in Stein finden wir in den Palästen der Königsstädte von Rajasthan in Nordindien. Das Ziel war für mich immer das Gleiche: Von diesen Marmorbauwerken lernen und das Gelernte in unsere moderne Architektur umsetzen. Ein Sprichwort sagt: „An der Zukunft gebaut – auf die Vergangenheit gestoßen.“ Diese Palastbauten zeigen den Weg auf, Ästhetisches in Geistiges zu transzendieren. Die persischen Kuppelbauten waren für mich schon immer von großem Interesse. Isfahan mit seinen Gärten, Brücken, Moscheen und Palästen inszeniert das Spiegelbild des Kosmos und des Paradieses zugleich. Die islamischen, geometrisch angelegten Gartenanlagen überformen die Natur zum Kunstwerk. Jede gute Architektur will eine Welt erschaffen, in der das Bauwerk ein mit Atmosphäre aufgeladenes Unikat ist. In Nordindien, in der Region Rajasthan, ist das Baumaterial der Paläste weißer Marmor. Mit ihm wurden leichte, durchscheinende, kosmisch wirkende Wandöffnungen geschaffen. Endlose Raumübergänge und Raumdurchdringungen inszenieren ein meisterhaftes Spiel mit der Transparenz, so etwa in der Palastanlage von Fatepur Sikri bei Agra. Die Transparenz ermöglicht ein Hindurchsehen, sie macht Verhülltes wieder zugänglich und öffnet den Betrachter gleichsam zur Neugierde.

Traditional roof design in Brione, Ticino, Switzerland, unknown architect (photo 2000)
Santiago Calatrava: bus station, St. Gallen, Switzerland, 1985–1986 (photo 2000)

Elementare Dachgestalt in Brione, Tessin, Schweiz, anonyme Architektur (Foto 2000)
Santiago Calatrava: Busstation, St. Gallen, Schweiz, 1985–1986 (Foto 2000)

Encounters with Master Architects

Osaka-based architect Tadao Ando is a master of restraint whose buildings seem to emerge out of nothingness. His emphasis on simplicity leads to a stillness, which allows the beauty of the space to be experienced. As poet Eduard Mörike wrote, "A thing of beauty seems blessed in itself." Paying homage to nature, Ando often embeds built form into the earth. His work suggests a perfection in which the human element cannot disturb nature. It requires courage and clarity, an ethos, and a mindset to discover the natural in building, to work with the simplicity of concrete, and to examine old ways of thinking in a way that allows debate with the prevailing state of affairs. Everything here is undergoing constant metamorphosis and is a reflection of the seeing eye and the thinking brain.

The potency of Santiago Calatrava's work is based on the diversity of his sphere of activities, which includes structural engineering, architecture, furniture design, and sculpture. His linguistic abilities are also impressive: he speaks Swedish with his wife, Italian with his father-in-law, and Swiss dialect with his children. For him, architecture is a unity of structural analysis and art. It is an object of structural engagement and at the same time a subject in the form of an artistic design. His buildings reflect his ability to extract rational solutions from complex relationships between structural engineering and architecture. His approach entails making structural features visible and, in the process, investing objects with their own aesthetic.

Norman Foster's aspiration to extreme elegance in glass and steel constructions speaks to the human yearning for harmony and beauty. Central to his approach is the endeavor to forge a powerful duality between construction and architecture. Empathy is one of the most important interpersonal experiences – in particular when it comes to the relationship between people who are fascinated with architecture. It was therefore particularly gratifying for me to be able to present current projects by a world-famous architect in the form of his working sketches. The large-format book *Norman Foster: Sketches* shows how the sketching of objects can expand the awareness of architecture. That being said, Foster is also a technology enthusiast, who delights in flying his helicopter above London. He flew to the Basel Architecture Lectures in a jet aircraft with his co-pilot. Since our budget was limited, I did not ask him about his expenses. However, it must be said that he did not enquire about my costs when I travelled to London.

The Swiss architect Theo Hotz is one of the most progressive architects of his generation. His choice of material, technique, and the idea of overall architecture he has promoted since the beginning of his career have made his work an expression of technical perfection. In 1999, the Swiss Federal Institute of Technology (ETH) in Zurich awarded him an honorary doctorate for his achievements. In person, Hotz is funny, ironic, generous, and genial. As an avant-garde architect, he developed the curtain wall in aesthetic, functional, and structural terms back in the 1950s. This opening of the outer shell creates freedom for movement in the interior space and simultaneously a feeling for the larger scale.

Other architects worthy of mention here include Jacques Herzog and Pierre de Meuron from Basel. The duo established a two-man office in the 1970s in the rear building at 80 St. Alban-Vorstadt, where I also had my office for a long time. Since then they have become world-renowned practitioners of their profession.

Richard Meier's concept is based on the idea of characterizing buildings externally through the systematic use of white. This restrained white appearance lends his structures a timeless, delicate elegance and is particularly effective in the case of museum buildings, the interiors of which also reflect this open mind-set. Meier's interior spaces are characterized by a remarkable sensitivity: at once light and dark, open and closed, functional and meditative. Art connoisseurs and patrons marvel at the seemingly natural juxtaposition of interdisciplinary exhibition spaces with glazed entrances and relaxation areas, an effect achieved by defining spatial groups in terms of luminosity, clarity, and determinacy. A bright zone is enclosed by dark space, engendering a sensation that is both intimate (conducive to concentration) and expansive (conducive to contemplation). The use of white brightens and expands the space, making it both mysterious and celebratory. My many encounters with Richard Meier's work, from villas to administration buildings, have been enriching experiences, not least because of Meier's ability to create an architecture that speaks to a broad public.

Begegnungen mit Meisterarchitekten

Tadao Ando, in Osaka lebend, ist ein Meister der Zurückhaltung, der aus dem Nichts seine Architektur entwickelt. Die auf das Einfache zielende Stimmung führt zur Stille, lässt die Schönheit der Leere erleben. Nach Eduard Mörike: „Was aber schön ist, selig scheint es in ihm selbst.“ Der Natur huldigend, vertieft Ando Bauformen in die Erde. Hier zeigt sich eine Vollendung, wenn alles Menschliche die Natur nicht stören kann. Es braucht Mut und Klarheit, Gesinnung und Haltung, um im Bauen das Natürliche zu entdecken, mit der Schlichtheit des Betons umzugehen und das alte Denken so aufbrechen, dass die Auseinandersetzung auf dem heutigen Stand stattfinden kann. Alles ist hier in ständiger Metamorphose, ist Reflexion des sehenden Auges und des denkenden Hirns.

Die Stärke von Santiago Calatrava liegt in der Vielfalt seines Tätigkeitbereichs. Sie reicht von der Ingenieurkunst zur Baukunst und vom Möbelentwurf zur Raumplastik. Aber auch sein Sprachtalent ist bemerkenswert: Mit seiner Frau Robertina spricht er Schwedisch, mit seinem Schwiegervater Italienisch und mit seinen Kindern den Schweizer Dialekt. Baukunst ist bei ihm eine Einheit zwischen Statik und Kunst. Sie ist Objekt der konstruktiven Auseinandersetzung und zugleich Subjekt als künstlerische Gestalt. In seinen Werken ist es ihm gelungen, komplizierte Zusammenhänge der Ingenieur- und Baukunst verständlich zu lösen. Er hat sich die Aufgabe gestellt, konstruktive Merkmale sichtbar zu machen, und gab damit dem Gegenstand seine eigene Ästhetik.

Das Streben von Norman Foster nach äußerster Eleganz in den Glas- und Stahlkonstruktionen entspricht der Sehnsucht des Menschen nach Harmonie und Schönheit. Sein größtes Anliegen ist es, zwischen Konstruktion und Architektur eine kraftvolle Dualität zu erzielen. Sympathie ist eine der wichtigsten zwischenmenschlichen Erfahrungen – insbesondere im Verhältnis zweier Menschen zueinander, die beide von Architektur fasziniert sind. So war es für mich eine besondere Freude, aktuelle Projekte eines weltberühmten Architekten mit seinen Skizzenarbeiten vorstellen zu dürfen. Das großformatige Buch „Norman Foster Sketches“ zeigt, wie gegenständliches Skizzieren das Bewusstsein von Architektur erweitern kann. Doch Norman Foster ist auch ein Technikbegeisterter, wenn er seinen Helikopter in 300 Metern Höhe über London steuert.

Zu den Basler Architektur-Vorträgen kam er mit Jet und Co-Pilot. Da unser Budget begrenzt war, fragte ich ihn nicht nach seinem Aufwand. Er erkundigte sich aber auch nie nach meinen Kosten, wenn ich nach London kam.

Der Schweizer Theo Hotz ist einer der progressivsten Architekten seiner Generation. Material, Technik und die Idee der Gesamtarchitektur, die er von Anfang an vermittelte, machten sein Werk zum Ausdruck seiner handwerklich-technischen Perfektion. Für dieses Bauschaffen bekam er 1999 den Dr. h. c. der ETH Zürich. Sein Charakter ist humorvoll-ironisch, großzügig-genial. Als avantgardistischer Baumeister hat er schon in den fünfziger Jahren die „Curtain Wall“ ästhetisch, funktionell und konstruktiv weiter entwickelt. Diese Öffnung der Außenhaut schafft reale Bewegungsfreiheit im Innenraum und weckt gleichzeitig das Gefühl eines großen Maßstabs.

Architekten, die auch in diese Reihe gehören, sind die Basler Jacques Herzog und Pierre de Meuron, die schon in den siebziger Jahren zu zweit ihr Büro gründeten, im Hinterhaus der St. Alban-Vorstadt 80, wo auch ich lange Zeit mein Büro hatte, und die seitdem ihre große Berufung zur Architektur entfaltet haben.

Das Konzept von Richard Meier folgt der Idee, Bauten durch ein konsequent in Weiß gehaltenes Erscheinungsbild zu prägen. Besonders im Museumsbau ergibt dieses zurückhaltende Weiß eine zeitlos grazile Eleganz. Diese offene Geisteshaltung spiegelt sich auch im Gebäude wider. So entstehen Innenräume mit einprägsamer Sensibilität: hell und dunkel, offen und geschlossen, zweckmäßig und meditativ zugleich. Kunstkenner und Kunstförderer bewundern dieses selbstverständliche Nebeneinander von interdisziplinären Ausstellungsräumen mit verglasten Zugängen und Erholungszonen. Es sind Raumgruppen, die durch Helligkeit, Klarheit und Bestimmtheit gekennzeichnet sind. Die helle Zone wird vom dunklen Raum umschlossen, und es entsteht eine Gefühl von Enge (Konzentration) und Weite (Kontemplation). Das Weiß macht den Raum lichter und weiter, geheimnisvoll und feierlich. In vielen Begegnungen war es für mich eine Bereicherung, seine Bauwerke von der Villa zum Verwaltungsgebäude zu erleben und zugleich zu sehen, wie er seine Architektur einer breiten Öffentlichkeit zu vermitteln versteht.

In 1994, the Australian architect Glenn Murcutt held a speech at the Basel Architecture Lectures, in which he told his audience that he only works on his commissions in the order he receives them. As a result, he has a waiting list of clients, which can be a source of irritation for those eager for his services. Although his practice is confined to a one-man office, Murcutt was awarded the renowned Pritzker Architecture Prize in 2002. A particularly notable aspect of his work is the architecture he has created for, and in close consultation with, Australian Aboriginal clients.

Portugal is a country on the edge of Europe. The city of Porto on the coast north of Lisbon is home to the architect Eduardo Souto de Moura, the renowned creator of purist, atmospheric buildings. Souto de Moura has an extraordinary facility for translating the stonemasonry tradition into abstract-modern structural forms. The cosmopolitan character of the local granite he uses draws the gaze as one approaches his buildings. In a conversation he once told me, "I began more or less at zero and focused on the essential elements of architecture." Granite has become a means by which he realizes his own particular vision of building: stone on stone.

My two books on the work of Renzo Piano, *Renzo Piano – Fondation Beyeler* and *Renzo Piano – Centre Kanak: Cultural Centre of the Kanak People*, represent highlights for me. In both works architecture links beauty and sensuousness with the life of the mind. A master of his craft, Piano has an appealing way of making a virtue of necessity. His messages are surprising, astute, highly logical, and always serve his overall intent. I was able to meet with him in his offices in Paris and Genoa and accompanied him to the Pritzker Architecture Prize award ceremony in Washington in 1998. The name of his firm, Renzo Piano Building Workshop, rightfully makes a claim to the construction *métier*.

In 1953, I spent Chinese New Year in Boston with I. M. Pei and his friends, the Chang siblings. We spoke about the relationship between the Far East and Western modernity. I encountered Pei again in Washington at a dinner held at the White House by President Bill Clinton and his wife Hillary. As a master architect working at the interface between Eastern and Western cultures, Pei has shown a rare ability to communicate his professional self-conception in clear and concrete terms.

Arthur Rüegg is a unique personality and a retired professor of architecture from the Swiss Federal Institute of Technology (ETH) in Zurich. He devised the concept for my book *Joint and Connection* (1992), thereby lending a clear form to the development of my work as a furniture designer. My aim has been to use my early training as a craftsman to develop well-engineered and patentable furniture. This book offers a kind of system for making furniture that covers the full range of geometric construction possibilities.

My monograph about Jakob Schilling, *Planning and Building,* documents an everyday type of architecture that is sustainable, durable, and cost-efficient. Schilling's professional rigor is a good example for the architecture profession. His ability as a builder speaks directly to people and invests his work with sense of beauty and dignity. Schilling is part of a generation of Swiss architects who, influenced by the modernism of the 1930s, have found their own path to a responsible form of building.

Peter Zumthor comes from a craft background and has been awarded numerous major international architecture prizes. He originally trained as a carpenter in the Basel region and has developed a singular approach to architecture based in part on his research into the structural forms characteristic of alpine valleys. His work addresses the social aspects of building and evokes associations with local cultural traditions, integrating aspects of contemporary building design, while never losing a sense of the mystery of his vocation. His outstanding designs are shaped by his life and connection with the alpine valleys in the canton of Graubünden. Drawing on traditional techniques, he developed a distinctive extension for the historical Gugalun House near Versam in Graubünden, an excellent contemporary example of how a centuries-old building can be given new life.

Ernst Koller (1900–2002) was an inventor and design engineer from Basel. Taking the formal canon of the Bauhaus architects as his starting point, he modernized metal construction techniques. His central thesis was that construction in the broadest sense constituted a fundamental element of design. The way a building was built determined its aesthetic quality and its beauty. He remained a design engineer and a businessman until he turned one hundred years old!

Im Jahre 1994 hielt der australische Architekt Glenn Murcutt eine Rede bei den Basler Architektur-Vorträgen. Er berichtete, dass seine Bauaufträge genau nach dem Datum der Bestellung eingeordnet werden. Als Folge davon entsteht in seinem Einmannbüro eine Warteliste, welche bei den Kunden auch Ärger erzeugt. Doch vor einigen Jahren wurde er trotz seines Einmannbüros mit dem renommierten Pritzker-Preis ausgezeichnet. Eine Besonderheit seines Schaffens ist seine Architektur und damit sein Verständnis für die Australischen Aborigines.

Ein Land am Rande von Europa ist Portugal. Dort finden wir in Porto den Architekten Eduardo Souto de Moura mit seinen puristisch-stimmungsvollen Bauten. Er versteht es hervorragend, die Steinmetztradition in abstrakt-moderne Bauformen zu verwandeln. Das durchaus Weltoffene des heimischen Granitsteins zieht beim Herannahen den Blick auf sich. Im Gespräch sagte er mir: „Ich begann quasi bei null und habe mich auf das Essenzielle in der Architektur konzentriert." Die Granitsteine wurden ihm zum Mittel, um die eigene Vorstellung vom Bauen zu verwirklichen: Stein auf Stein.

Meine beiden Bücher über Renzo Piano „Beyeler Museum" und „Kulturzentrum der Kanak in Nouméa" (Neukaledonien) waren Highlights. In beiden Werken verbindet die Architektur das Schöne und das Sinnliche mit dem Geistigen. Ein Meister wie Piano macht auf sympathische Weise aus Nöten eine Tugend. Seine Pointen kommen überraschend, mit Scharfsinn und bestechlicher Logik, und dienen nur der Sache. Ich durfte ihn in seinen Büros in Paris und Genua treffen und zur Pritzker-Preisübergabe 1998 in Washington begleiten. Der Name seiner Firma „Renzo Piano Building Workshop" weist zu Recht den Anspruch des baumeisterlichen „Metiers" aus.

Das chinesische Neujahr 1953 verbrachte ich in Boston mit I. M. Pei und seinen Freunden, dem Geschwisterpaar Chang. Wir sprachen über das Spannungsfeld zwischen dem Fernen Osten und unserer westlichen Moderne. Erneut begegnet ich Pei bei einem Dinner im „White House" in Washington, in Anwesenheit des US-amerikanischen Präsidenten Bill Clinton und seiner Frau Hillary. Selten hat ein Meisterarchitekt sein berufliches Selbstverständnis zwischen den beiden Kulturen Orient und Okzident so realitätsnah zu überliefern verstanden wie Pei.

Eine ganz eigene Persönlichkeit ist Arthur Rüegg, emeritierter Professor für Architektur an der ETH Zürich. Er hat mein Buch „Fügen und Verbinden" (1992) inszeniert und so der Arbeit meiner Möbelentwicklung eine klare Gestalt gegeben. Mein Ziel war es ja, auf der Basis meiner handwerklichen Grundausbildung konstruktive und patentfähige Möbel zu entwickeln. Das Buch bietet nun eine Art Systematik im Möbelbau, welche die vielfältigen Möglichkeiten der geometrischen Konstruktion auszuschöpfen weiß.

Meine Monografie „Planen und Bauen" über Jakob Schilling dokumentiert eine ernst zu nehmende Alltagsarchitektur: haltbar, lange Zeit benutzbar, ressourcenschonend, kostengünstig. Schillings Tatkraft tut der Architektur gut. Seine Baumeisterlichkeit spricht unmittelbar zum Menschen und erzeugt ein Gefühl von Schönheit, Würde und Eindrücklichkeit. Schilling ist Teil einer Schweizer Architektengeneration, welche, beeinflusst von der Moderne der dreißiger Jahre, einen eigenen Weg zum verantwortungsvollen Bauen gefunden hat.

Peter Zumthor, das vom Handwerk her kommende und mit vielen großen internationalen Architekturpreisen ausgezeichnete Talent, lernte das Metier des Handwerks in der Basler Region und recherchierte die Bauformen der Alpentäler, um daraus seinen eigenen Stil zu entwickeln. Er greift das einfach Soziale auf, weckt Assoziationen zum heimischen Volksgut, legt deutliche Spuren zum heutigen Bauen und verliert doch das Geheimnis seiner Berufung nicht. Sein Leben und seine Verbundenheit mit den Alpentälern im Kanton Graubünden prägen seine perfekte Gestaltung. Dort hat er seinen eigenen, aus der Tradition stammenden „Strick" für das Haus „Gugalun" bei Versam (Graubünden) entwickelt: wohl das Beste, wie eine über ein Jahrhundert alte Gestalt zu neuem Leben erweckt werden kann.

Ernst Koller (1900–2002) war ein Erfinder und Konstrukteur aus Basel. Vom Formenkanon der Bauhausarchitekten ausgehend, modernisierte er die Metallbautechnik. Dabei ging es ihm um die zentrale These, dass Konstruktion im weitesten Sinne ein grundlegendes Element der Gestaltung ist. Die Technik eines Gebäudes bestimmt dessen ästhetische Qualität, seine Schönheit. Er war und blieb ein Konstrukteur und Unternehmer, eine findige und erfinderische Persönlichkeit bis ins hundertste Lebensjahr.

Tadao Ando: Vitra Training Center, Weil am Rhein, Germany, 1992–1993
Front perspective and photo (photo 2000)

Tadao Ando: Vitra Training Center, Weil am Rhein, Deutschland, 1992–1993
Frontalperspektive und Foto (Foto 2000)

I. M. Pei: Glass pyramid, entrance to the Louvre, Paris, 1987/88 (photo 1990)
Ancient observatory of Dengfeng (Dengfeng gu guanxiangtai) in Henan province, 13th century (photo 2005)

I. M. Pei: Glaspyramide, Eingang zum Louvre, Paris, 1987/88 (Foto 1990)
Altes Observatorium von Dengfeng (Dengfeng gu guanxiangtai), Provinz Henan, China, 13. Jahrhundert (Foto 2005)

Artistic Inspiration

In 1956, I met the artist Josef Albers, a former teacher at the Weimar and Dessau Bauhaus. We agreed on an exchange: his painting *Homage to the Square* (blue and ochre version) in exchange for two of my “all in line” steel tube cantilever chairs. Several years later, I had the pleasure of meeting with him again in his house in New Haven, Connecticut, along with his wife, Anni Albers, a well-known textile artist.

Constantin Brâncusi, an artist I have long admired, was born into a peasant family in Hobiţa, Romania. He lived in Paris, yet in his work and life remained closely tied to his peasant roots. His sculptures exhibit an extraordinary simplicity and symbolic power. Whether working in wood, marble, or metal, he invested archaic forms with a classical purity, interweaving the spiritual and the material in works such as *Colonne sans fin* (1937) in Târgu Jiu, Romania. Brâncusi took the path of East-West migration and created a body of work that compels us to traverse this path in the opposite direction. One of his central tenets is summed up in the statement, “Beauty is absolute balance.”

On the tongue of land where San Sebastian stretches furthest into the sea on the Bay of Biscay, three iron sculptures by Eduardo Chillida entitled *Peines del Viento* (1977) are framed by a spatial design by Chillida and Luis Peña Ganchegui. In 1988, on the recommendation of Santiago Calatrava, Chillida invited a group of my friends and I to meet him there. In the context of the architectural frame provided by a minimally equipped platform and the surrounding ocean, his sculptures became comprehensible. The triad of nature, primal form, and landscape design exerted a powerful effect. We subsequently accompanied Chillida back to his apartment on the hillside leading down to the ocean and, from there, to Donostia and his studio in the countryside. Later, in 1990, he took part in a symposium at the Basel Architecture Lectures, where we were able to witness the openness and engagement of this extremely amiable man, who treasures relationships.

The De Stijl movement, which was active in Amsterdam from 1917 to 1931, has been another source of inspiration for my own work. I was able to acquire original pieces of furniture by the Utrecht-based craftsman, G. A. van de Groenekan, Gerrit Rietveld’s authorized master carpenter, and thus to build up my own Rietveld collection. De Stijl connected technical functionalism with aesthetic constructivism and saw the aesthetic value of a form as more than a consequence of function. The resulting aesthetic is delicate and light and recalls the Japanese tea ceremony furniture created by Zen Buddhists in Kyoto from the sixteenth century onwards.

The wood sculptor Wilhelm Münger from Basel created his works with a band saw. Trained as a carpenter (like Brâncusi), his fascination with wood brought him to art. Forging a link between purpose and beauty was his technical credo. His mathematically proportioned sculptures give rise to an aesthetic manifestation that is comparable to never-ending poetry. His works aim to develop the mathematical in a way that is spiritual and meditative, while at the same time orientated to the concrete world, thereby giving expression to an inner force that is like a yearning for beauty.

The *Picture Objects* created by Nelly Rudin, who lived in Zurich, chart an overall development that saw this trained graphic designer transform herself into an artist. In Rudin’s contemporary art, and especially in her concrete art, the true becomes visible through a reduction to the essential. The most conspicuous result of her artistic interventions in her *Picture Objects* is what is grasped, recognized, and produced – her minimalism has an intensely sensuous quality that continues to present a comprehensive challenge. Since her death in 2013, the Nelly Rudin Foundation, run by Jakob Bill, Theodor Steinmann, and myself, has assumed stewardship of her work.

Im Kreis der Kunst leben

Mit dem Maler und Meister am Bauhaus Weimar und Dessau, Josef Albers, den ich 1956 an der Hochschule in Ulm kennen lernte, kam ein Tausch zustande: sein Bild „Hommage to the Square" (eine blau-ocker Version) gegen zwei meiner Stahlrohr-Sessel, die Freischwinger „all in Line". Einige Jahre danach begegnete ich ihm wieder in seinem Haus in New Haven, Connecticut, mit seiner Frau Anni Albers, einer bekannten Textilkünstlerin.

Ein von mir verehrter Künstler war Constantin Brâncusi, geboren in einem Hirtenhaus im rumänischen Hobiţa. Er lebte in Paris, blieb jedoch in seinem Werk und Leben mit seiner bäuerlichen Heimat eng verbunden. Seine Plastiken zeugen von außergewöhnlicher Einfachheit und Symbolkraft. Aus dem Wesen der Materie, sei es aus Holz, Marmor oder Metall, hat er archaische Formen in klassischer Reinheit zum Klingen gebracht. Geistiges und Materielles durchdringen sich. Wir denken an die „Colonne sans fin" von 1937 im Park von Târgu Jiu in Rumänien. Brâncusi hat den Weg der Ost-West-Wanderung gemacht. Und wir müssen ihn umgekehrt zurücklegen. Seine prägende Aussage: „Das Schöne ist das absolut Ausgeglichene."

Am äußersten Zipfel von San Sebastian, am Golf von Biskaya, stehen im Meer drei Eisenskulpturen „Peines del Viento" (1977) von Eduardo Chillida, umrahmt von der Platzgestaltung einer Gemeinschaftsarbeit mit Luis Peña Ganchegui. Dorthin hat Chillida meine Freunde und mich, auf Empfehlung von Santiago Calatrava, 1988 zu einem Rendezvous eingeladen. Im Kontext der bestehenden Architektur, einer auf ein Minimum ausgerichteten Plattform, und der umgebenden Meer-Natur, wurden seine Skulpturen verständlich. Der Dreiklang von Natur, Urform und Landschaftsgestaltung war gewaltig. Dann ging es zurück in sein Wohnhaus, am Hang und dem Meer zugewandt, und von dort nach Donostia zu seinem Atelier in der Landschaft. Später, 1990, gastierte er bei einem Symposium der Basler Architektur-Vorträge in der Kunsthalle. Der überaus sympathische Mann, dem Beziehungen so wichtig sind, ist bei Gesprächen stets mit aller Offenheit präsent.

Auch durch die holländische „De Stijl"-Bewegung, 1917–1931 in Amsterdam, bekam ich viele Anregungen für meine Arbeit. Von Gerrit Rietvelds autorisiertem Tischlermeister, G. A. van de Groenekan aus Utrecht, konnte ich originale Möbel beziehen und so eine eigene Rietveld-Sammlung aufbauen. Diese Stühle wurden vielfach mit sichtbar verdübelten Vierkanthölzern entwickelt. Der ästhetische Wert einer Form wurde nicht nur als Folge der Funktion gesehen, sondern parallel zum technischen Funktionalismus mit einem ästhetischen Konstruktivismus in Verbindung gebracht. Die neue Ästhetik, ihre grazile Leichtigkeit, hat eine bestechende Nähe zu den japanischen Teezeremonien-Möbeln, einer Kreation der Zen-Buddhisten in Kyoto seit dem 16. Jahrhundert.

Der Holzbildhauer Wilhelm Münger aus Basel entwickelte seine Werke mit der Bandsäge. Den gelernten Schreiner (wie Brâncusi) hat die Faszination von Holz zur Kunst geführt. Sein handwerkliches Credo ist es, Zweck und Schönheit miteinander zu verbinden. Seine Sinusskulpturen lassen eine ästhetische Ausprägung entstehen, die als geistige Schöpfung einer nie verstummenden Poesie gleichkommt: sie wollen das Mathematische geistig-meditativ und zugleich welthaltig entwickeln und bringen so eine innere Kraft zum Ausdruck wie eine Sehnsucht nach Schönheit.

Die Bildobjekte von Nelly Rudin, die aus Basel stammt und in Zürich gelebt hat, zeigen eine ganzheitliche Entwicklung, in der sich die gelernte Grafikerin zur Künstlerin wandelte. In der Gegenwartskunst, und besonders in ihrer konkreten Kunst, wird das Wahre durch die Reduktion auf das Wesentliche sichtbar. Das augenfälligste Ergebnis ihrer künstlerischen Eingriffe in den Bildobjekten ist das Be-griffene, Er-kannte, Her-gestellte – ihr Minimalismus besitzt eine hohe sinnliche Qualität, die auch weiterhin eine umfassende Herausforderung darstellt. Seit ihrem Tode 2013 nimmt sich die „Nelly Rudin-Stiftung", mit Jakob Bill (Präsident), Theodor Steinmann und mir, ihrer Sache an.

Success in Competitions

We take part in competitions in order to win. It is always a great challenge when invention and production are unified in a creative act that not only generates something new, but also seeks to gain recognition.

The International Competition of the Museum of Modern Art in New York (MoMA) in 1948 was the first furniture competition for which I received recognition – from a jury that included Mies van der Rohe. Further recognition came in 1952, when I won an award for my tea table with a visible cross foot at the Good Design competition held by MoMA in New York with a jury that included Edward Kaufmann and Charles Eames. Unfortunately, as I learned from a conversation in Chicago with Hans Knoll, a native of Stuttgart who owned a furniture firm, production technology in the USA could not offer the precision required for the visible cross foot. In addition, my floor lamp was included as an exhibition object in the Good Design collection shown by MoMA New York.

In 1955 and 1957, my wood-joint furniture was awarded the first and ex aequo et bono prize at the *Concorso Internazionale del Mobile* in Cantù, Italy. With Alvar Aalto on the jury, I saw this recognition as my greatest success in the sense that I had taken timber jointing to the level of an artwork.

It was through my connection with Cantù that I met the lawyer Dr. Hans Deichmann from Inverigo near Como. He worked for Helmut von Moltke, the German resistance fighter's family. Deichmann's support for my involvement in the competition was an enormous help.

I also met James Prestini, an Italian engineer and professor, who taught at the Illinois Institute of Technology. His hobby was woodturning and he became well-known as a producer of high-quality wooden salad bowls. Prestini was awarded a prize at the International Low-Cost Furniture Design Competition held by MoMA in 1952.

Wettbewerbserfolge

An Wettbewerben beteiligt man sich, um zu gewinnen. Es ist immer eine große Herausforderung, wenn sich das Erfinden und Schaffen zu einem schöpferischen Tun vereinigt, das nicht nur Neues hervorbringt, sondern auch als solches Anerkennung finden will: Sie gibt Hoffnung.

„The International Competition of the Museum of Modern Art" in New York (MoMA) 1948 war der erste Möbelwettbewerb, bei dem ich eine Anerkennung bekommen habe, mit Mies van der Rohe in der Jury. Bei einem weiteren Wettbewerb 1952 für „Good Design" vom MoMA NY mit Edward Kaufmann und Charles Eames als Juroren wurde mein Teetisch mit sichtbarem Kreuzfuss ausgewählt. Bei einem Gespräch in Chicago mit dem Möbelfirma-Inhaber Hans Knoll aus Stuttgart ergab sich leider, dass die Präzision des in der Tischplatte sichtbaren Kreuzfusses in der erforderlichen präzisen Herstellungstechnik in den USA nicht möglich ist. Auch meine Stehlampe wurde in die Collection „Good Design" vom MoMA New York als Ausstellungsobjekt integriert.

Meine Möbelentwicklung in Holzfügungen wurde im „Concorso Internazionale del Mobile" in Cantù 1955 und 1957 mit dem ersten und Ex-aequo-Preis prämiert. Es war (mit Alvar Aalto in der Jury) mein grösster Erfolg, indem Holzverbindungen zum Kunstwerk erhoben wurden.

In Zusammenhang mit Cantù lernte ich den Rechtsanwalt Dr. Hans Deichmann aus Inverigo in der Nähe von Como (Italien) kennen. Er gehörte zur Familie von Helmut von Moltke, dem Widerstandskämpfer aus Deutschland. Seine Unterstützung zur Realisierung des Wettbewerbs war mir eine große Hilfe.

Weiter begegnete ich James Prestini, einem italienischen Ingenieur und Professor, der am Illinois Institute of Technology Chicago lehrte. Bekannt war er durch sein Hobby: das Drechseln von erstklassigen Holzsalatschüsseln, und als Preisträger vom „International Low-Cost Furniture Design Competition" vom MoMA NY 1952.

Habit – Habitat

Furniture, architecture, and journalism were the three professional branches to which I devoted myself in the following years, translating what I had learned into my own works. I designed furniture and lamps and was the architect of residential buildings, public buildings, and a space-framework storage depot. The third branch, producing books, came about as a way of using my time productively during periods when I had no architectural commissions to work on. In the area of furniture design, my prototypes, even if they did not go into mass production, found recognition for their inventiveness and aesthetic expressiveness. Building brought me recognition in terms of both construction and design.

The fact that I did not actively seek clients meant that I had fewer commissions than others. The following is a summary of my body of work as an architect:

- Bromhübel cemetery complex in Arlesheim with a relief of a cross in the brick wall of the funeral hall
- Müllheim children's home, a children's village with pavilions using a skeleton construction
- Development plan for Tüllingen children's home with school and residential pavilions
- Residential buildings in Bottmingen, two identical dwellings of corten steel and exposed brick
- Hexagonal free-plan dwellings in Biel-Benken, glazed on all facades
- Casa Nascosta with wooden veranda and loggia, which invigorated the pre-existing stone architecture in Ascona
- Storage depot in Märkt, a space framework with the ability for extension
- Kindergarten in Bottmingen
- Hexagonal houses in the Jura
- Design of the Barfüsserplatz public square in Basel

A great deal of my time has been absorbed by producing books addressing international topics and with the development of furniture based on timber joinery. A more recent aspect of my work involves the creation of collages using my photos and thus reflecting the past in a contemporary manner.

To strive for good design has been central to all my projects. The search for the truth of good buildings, so to speak, has been a focus throughout my career. Good buildings have an illuminating and embracing effect. An architecture characterized by simplicity, composure, and human urbanity is timeless and does not age. The development of a good design, from material to proportions, is a challenging process, with which I have wrestled for long periods during the course of my career. Seriousness is an essential aspect here, for I believe one of the essences of good design is attitude.

People are born to dwell. Our skin, our clothes, and our home are the three protective coverings in, and with which we live. This concept is alluded to, for example, by *Lebenshüllen* (mantles of life) by the Zurich clothes designer, Christa de Carouge, whose clothes are featured in my book *Habit – Habitat*. Everywhere in the world, we find elemental forms of dwelling whose designs express the feeling for the life of their builders and inhabitants. They have, in turn, provided sources of inspiration for new work for me and many other designers.

Establishing a tradition was also the point of departure for the touring exhibition "70/80 Architecture in Switzerland," which I developed in 1980 for the Pro Helvetica cultural foundation. Using thirty examples from German-, French-, and Italian-speaking Swiss cantons, this exhibition documented the living tradition of modern architecture in Switzerland. It was exhibited in eighty countries throughout the world. From 1981–1984 there were even two multilingual, identical versions of the exhibition in circulation: one in Europe, the others in North and South America, and the Far East.

Habit – Habitat

Möbel, Architektur und Publizistik waren die drei Berufszweige, welchen ich mich in den folgenden Jahren widmete. Das Gelernte wurde in eigene Arbeiten übertragen. Im Design waren es Möbel und Lampen, in der Architektur Wohnhäuser, öffentliche Bauten und eine Lagerhalle in Raumfachwerk. Der dritte Zweig – jener der Bücher – entstand eigentlich als Zeitfüller, wenn keine Architekturaufträge zu bewältigen waren. Im Möbeldesign bekamen meine Prototypen, auch wenn ihnen der Weg zum Herstellverfahren versagt blieb, gute Noten im erfinderischen und ästhetischen Gestaltausdruck. Das Bauen brachte mir Anerkennung in Bezug auf Konstruktion und Gestalt.

Da ich keine Kundenwerbung machte, hatte ich dementsprechend weniger Aufträge. Hier eine Zusammenfassung meines Arbeitsvolumens als Architekt:

- Friedhofanlage Bromhübel in Arlesheim mit Kreuzrelief im Backsteinverband in der Abdankungshalle
- Kinderheim Müllheim, ein Kinderdorf mit Pavillons in Skelettkonstruktion
- Bebauungsplan für das Kinderheim Tüllingen mit Schule und Wohnungspavillons
- Wohnhaus in Bottmingen, zwei gleiche Häuser in Cortenstahl und Sichtbackstein
- Sechseck-Wohnhäuser in Biel-Benken mit freiem Grundriss, allseits verglast
- Casa Nascosta mit Holzveranda und Loggia, welche die vorhandene Steinarchitektur beleben, in Ascona
- Lagerhalle in Märkt (D), ein Raumfachwerk mit Erweiterungsmöglichkeiten.
- Kindergarten in Bottmingen
- Sechseckhäuser im Jura
- Platzgestaltung Barfüsserplatz in Basel

Meine Hauptarbeit konzentrierte sich auf Bücher über internationale Themen und die Möbelentwicklung von Fügen und Verbindung. Eine neue Arbeitsweise ist es schließlich, Collagen aus eigenen Fotos zu entwickeln und so Vergangenes im Gegenwärtigen zu spiegeln.

Bei allen Projekten stand für mich die gute Gestaltung im Vordergrund. Der Wahrheit guter Bauwerke ins Gesicht zu sehen, diese Perspektive hat sich bei mir bis heute erhalten. Gute Bauwerke wirken einleuchtend und offen. Alles lebt. Eine Architektur, welche Einfachheit, Gelassenheit und das menschliche Urbane in sich hat, altert nicht. Die Entwicklung einer guten Gestalt, vom Material bis zur Proportionsfindung, ist ein Prozess: Oft habe ich selbst lange mit mir gerungen. Dabei ist die Ernsthaftigkeit ein wesentlicher Faktor. Denn die Essenz guter Gestaltung ist Haltung.

Der Mensch ist zum Wohnen geboren: Unsere Haut, unser Kleid, unser Haus, das sind die drei Hüllen, in und mit denen wir leben. Das zeigen etwa auch die „Lebenshüllen" der Kleidermacherin Christa de Carouge aus Zürich in meinem Buch „Habit – Habitat". Überall auf der Welt finden wir elementare Wohnformen, die in ihrer Gestaltung das Lebensgefühl ihrer Erbauer und Bewohner zum Ausdruck bringen. Zugleich waren diese Zeugen jedoch eine Inspirationsquelle für neue Arbeiten – von mir wie von anderen.

Tradition stiften war auch der Ausgangspunkt der Wanderausstellung „70/80 Architecture in Switzerland", einer Arbeit, die ich 1980 im Auftrag der Kulturstiftung Pro Helvetia entwickelt habe. Mit 30 Beispielen aus der Deutschschweiz, dem Welschland und dem Tessin dokumentierte diese Ausstellung die lebendige Tradition der modernen Architektur in der Schweiz. Sie wurde weltweit in über 80 Ländern gezeigt. Von 1981 bis 1984 zirkulierten sogar zwei mehrsprachige, identische Ausstellungen: eine in Europa, die andere auf dem amerikanischen Kontinent und im Fernen Osten.

Werner Blaser: Lüber storage depot in Märkt, Germany, Varitec framework used for the roof and facade, 1970–1971 (photo 1971)
Wooden construction in the open-air museum in Kiev, Ukraine (photo 1980)

Werner Blaser: Lagerhalle Lüber in Märkt, Deutschland, Raumfachwerk Varitec in Dach und Fassade, 1970–1971 (Foto 1971)
Holzkonstruktion aus dem Freilichtmuseum in Kiew, Ukraine (Foto 1980)

Art in the Details of Furniture

Many master architects of the twentieth century have designed furniture, most frequently chairs. A piece of furniture is, of course, also a part of a building. However, in contrast to the building as edifice, furniture is something extremely personal; it energizes both body and mind. Furniture, the little sister of the house, embodies everything a person needs in terms of intuitive feeling and experiences on a haptic level. A piece of furniture can be experienced by sight and touch. When developing my own furniture, my focus has been, above all, on the art of joinery. It is the join that crystallizes the laws of construction, and it is for this reason that joints are visible in the furniture I have developed. The visibility of the individual joint becomes what is characteristic about these objects: technical necessity attaining a clarity and beauty.

The visible aspect of construction is its all-embracing element. This principle has always been central to the development of my furniture and guided my design approach down to the smallest structural detail. This approach did not develop merely out of the search for form, but rather from a struggle with the limits of the possible in my endeavor to create a fusion of technical and aesthetic design with a refined intellectual foundation. Making the construction visible invests the object with texture, creating a design that enriches the piece with something beautiful and enduring.

Drawing on my training as a cabinetmaker, I developed the ability to devise constructional and patentable solutions, including the following:

1. Cross joint: a cross foot cut into two parts, subsequently used to create a cross foot from a profile beam consisting of four identical parts.
2. Triangle joint: a profile beam cut into three equal parts to form a triangle foot or triangle frame.
3. Slotted joint: with grooves and slits in a square beam.
4. Socket joint: three identical beams connected to form a three-dimensional cross.
5. Ridge joint: six boards cut with ridges to form a cube. The idea was to design my own "De Stijl" furniture based on "genuine" construction details.
6. Sheet joint: slotting and joining of plywood elements for demountable furniture such as chairs, table, and cabinets.

All joints with patent certificates can be used to develop complete furniture series.

Visible construction subsequently became my trademark. For me, joinery has always expressed the "built" character of a piece. My design work has never been a response to fashion; it is an expression and legacy of a particular time in which we live and create. One aim of my work over many years has been to foster an active awareness of the significance of void or empty space, a concept that Mies incorporated into Western modernism and one that Zen Buddhism has cultivated since the sixteenth century.

Kunst im Möbeldetail

Große Meisterarchitekten im 20. Jahrhundert haben sich mit der Möbelentwicklung beschäftigt, hauptsächlich mit Stühlen. Auch ein Möbel ist ja ein Bauwerk. Aber im Gegensatz zum Bauwerk ist das Möbel etwas ganz Persönliches. Es belebt Körper und Geist. Im Möbel, der kleinen Schwester des Hauses, liegt alles, was ein Mensch als Bauchgefühl braucht und haptisch erlebt. Im Sehen und Tasten kann ein Möbel erahnt werden. Beim Entwickeln meiner Möbel kam es mir vor allem auf die Kunst des Fügens an: An der Fuge kristallisiert sich die Gesetzlichkeit, und darum sind die Fugenstellen auch sichtbar. Die Sichtbarkeit der einzelnen Fugung wird zum Charakteristischen dieser Objekte: Was technisch notwendig ist, wirkt hier klar und schön.

Das Sichtbare der Konstruktion ist das Allumfassende. Weil mir diese Notwendigkeit bei meinen Möbelentwicklungen ständig gegenwärtig war, konnte ich die Durchführung der Konstruktionsidee am kleinsten Detail darlegen. Diese Arbeitsweise ist nicht aus bloßem Formgebungswillen entsprungen. Vielmehr war es ein Ringen um das, was in der Verbindung von technischem und ästhetischem Gestalten an der Grenze des Möglichen war und zugleich höchste geistige Qualität besitzt: Die Sichtbarmachung der Konstruktion soll dem Objekt das Gefüge geben; durch diese Gestaltung wird das Möbel mit etwas Schönem und Bleibendem bereichert.

Auf der Basis meiner handwerklichen Grundausbildung entwickelte ich die Fähigkeit, eigene konstruktive und patentfähige Lösungen am Möbel zu erarbeiten. Folgende Möbelentwicklungen habe ich dabei abgeschlossen:

1. Die Kreuzverbindung: ein in zwei Teile zerlegter Kreuzfuß. Später aus einem Profilstab in vier identische Teile zu einem Kreuzfuß zusammengeschoben.
2. Dreiecksverbindung: ein Profilstab, in drei gleiche Teile zum Dreiecksfuß oder zur Dreieckszarge zerlegt.
3. Schlitzverbindung: mit Nut und Schlitz im quadratischen Stab.
4. Steckverbindung: drei formgleiche, rechteckige Stäbe, zum räumlichen Kreuz verbunden.
5. Leistenverbindung: sechs Platten, mit Leisten zum Kubus zerlegt. Die Idee war, ein eigenes „De Stijl-Möbel“ in „wahren“ Konstruktionsdetails zu gestalten.
6. Plattenverbindung: Stecken und Verbinden von Sperrholzelementen zu zerlegbaren Möbeln wie Stuhl, Tisch und Kasten.

Aus allen Verbindungen mit Patenturkunden können jeweils vollständige Programme für Gebrauchsmöbel entwickelt werden.

In der Folge wurde die sichtbare Konstruktion zu meinem Emblem. Das Gefügte hatte für mich aber immer „Bau“-Charakter. Gestalten wurde nie zur Mode, eher zum Ausdruck und Vermächtnis unseres Zeitgeschehens. Ein Ziel meiner langjährigen Arbeit war es, die Bedeutung des leeren Raums, welche Mies in die westliche Moderne aufgenommen hat und die dem Zen-Buddhismus schon seit dem 16. Jahrhundert vertraut war, wieder aktiv bewusst zu machen.

Werner Blaser: Residential building with corten steel frame, Bottmingen, Basel-countryside, 1967–1969, with Rietveld furnishings (photo 1980)
Development of furniture: Werner Blaser, "Art of the Joint" series (photo 1955)

Werner Blaser: Wohnhaus in Corten-Stahlskelett, Bottmingen, Basel-Landschaft, 1967–1969, mit Rietveld-Möbel (Foto 1980)
Möbelentwicklung: Werner Blaser „Kunst der Fuge" (Foto 1955)

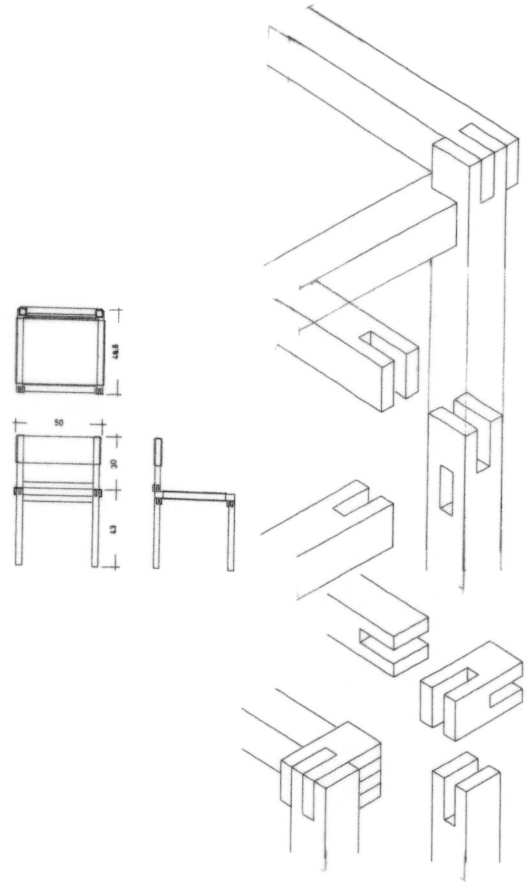

Photo Collage

I began taking photographs of architecture in Chicago in 1952 with an SLR camera in a 6 × 6 cm picture format and later used a Rollei 66. Photography was, in itself, good training for the composition of photo collages. But it was, above all, my research into traditional buildings in different parts of the world – from haylofts in the Alps to memorials in Kyoto – that led me to the development of my specific approach to collage.

The "Living Archive" at Blaser Architekten AG in Basel contains the collections "Mies van der Rohe in Chicago, 1952–69" and "Temple and Tea House," a study of classical buildings in Japan constructed from the sixteenth to the eighteenth century. These collections provided the source material for the photo collages presented here.

I began making collages before the turn of the millennium using the "papier déchiré" method. But did this traditional approach suffice? In recent years, collage has increasingly become my tool of choice. Gluing and overlapping photographs and tracing paper allows one to discern the "statement" of a design.

The collages offer an optical stimulus through which the beholder can bring together constructional possibilities in a context. In the pictorial "meditation," a totality of understanding and meaning emerges beyond all fashionable trends. The photo collage facilitates new ways of seeing. It reveals identical or similar elements shared by the pictorial worlds of modernism and classical Far Eastern architecture by accessing a level of feeling and empathy. In this way, a three-hundred-year history of Zen architecture becomes a synaesthetic experience in the present. We realize that in constructional and aesthetic terms, our Western modernism is connected to classical Japanese buildings, which continue to thrill and stimulate us.

Fazit der Fotocollage

Für meine Bücher konnte ich seit 1952 Chicago mit einer Spiegelreflexkamera und einem 6 × 6 cm großen Bildausschnitt fotografieren, später benutzte ich eine Rollei 66. Diese Aufnahmen waren eine gute Voraussetzung für Fotocollagen. Das weltweite Recherchieren tradierter Bauwerke gab mir den Anstoß, mein eigenes System beim Collagieren zu entwickeln: vom Heustadel in der Alpenregion bis zu den Denkmälern im japanischen Kyoto.

Im „Living Archive“ bei Blaser Architekten AG in Basel befindet sich nun eine vollständige Fotosammlung zu Mies van der Rohe in Chicago, 1952–1969, sowie zu den klassischen Bauten des 16.–18. Jahrhunderts, „Tempel und Teehaus“, in Japan. Sie waren die Voraussetzung für die hier vorgelegten Fotocollagen.

Mit dem Collagieren begann ich noch vor Ende des vergangenen Jahrhunderts: durch das Kleben von Fundstücken mittels „papier déchiré“. Genügte mir aber dieses traditionelle Verfahren in seiner üblichen Machbarkeit? Inzwischen ist das Collagieren mehr und mehr zu meinem Werkzeug geworden: Durch das Kleben und Übereinandergreifen von Fotografien und Pauspapier lässt sich die „Aussage“ einer Gestalt ermitteln.

Die Collagen bieten dem Beschauer einen optischen Reiz, durch den der Betrachter die konstruktiven Möglichkeiten in einen Zusammenhang bringen kann. In der Bild-„Meditation“ entsteht jenseits aller modischen Trends ein Ganzes für Verstand und Sinne. Die Fotocollage ermöglicht neue Sichtweisen: Sie deckt durch eine Tiefenschicht des Fühlens und Teilhabens Gleiches oder Ähnliches zwischen den Bildwelten der Moderne und den Klassikern fernöstlicher Architektur auf. Eine dreihundertjährige Geschichte der Zen-Architektur wird so in der Gegenwart zum synästhetischen Erlebnis. Wir erkennen, dass unsere Moderne in einer konstruktiven und ästhetischen Verbindung mit den klassischen japanischen Bauten steht, die uns nach wie vor begeistern und stimulieren.

Abbot Kobori Sohaku Daitoku-ji temple district (photo 1960)
Rice paper sliding doors, Kyoto, Japan (photo 1960)

Abt Kobori Sohaku im Daitôku-ji-Tempelbezirk (Foto 1960)
Schiebetür aus Reispapier, Kyoto, Japan (Foto 1960)

Home is Homeland

Homeland (Heimat) is home (Heim) and secret (Geheimnis) or: homeland is where the secret dwells. It is there that one experiences and senses what connects. My parents gave me confidence in my own abilities and for this reason I will be eternally grateful to them. Home represents the sedentary aspect of one's character, a place where one belongs and takes refuge. And as Goethe says in *Faust,* "That which you inherit from your fathers, you must earn in order to possess."

My directness, candor, and eagerness to get straight to the point are also qualities I learned from my parents. In the last phase of his working life, my father, Gottfried, was a police officer. He endeavored to guide my development, while at the same time allowed me the greatest degree of freedom. My mother, Katharina, a stylish dresser and homemaker, took a similar approach. She taught me to lead a healthy life and to maintain a positive attitude. My father, by contrast, was more introverted. Although money was never an issue, providing for four children required a certain degree of thrift.

I have been enormously lucky that I had my wife, Helen, at my side. Helen was a textile designer whose work integrated well with my own designs. As director of the textile course at the Basel School of Crafts (today the University of Applied Sciences) and an expert in the craft of handwoven tapestry, she was predestined to enliven by constructions with her art. For this reason, a weaving loom was an indispensable feature of my first office and, later, of our house in Bottmingen. Her work has shown me the connection between technology and art in a concrete way. The word "technology," which comes from the Greek word *techne*, meaning craftsmanship and embraces the idea of art: behind the essence of technology stands art. Following Helen's death in 2004, our son Christian presented her oeuvre in an exhibition held at his office. Our friends, along with former students, were invited to come and choose pieces of her work to keep as keepsakes. With this gift we have been able to ensure the preservation and enduring effect of her rich textile art.

The story of my life would not be complete without a mention of our son, Christian. As parents we reared him to play rather than learn. Yet play also includes planning and structure, and at the end of play there is the equally important aspect of clearing up in order to making a new beginning possible. Structure and arrangement belong together. This "play" is repeated on a daily basis now when he, as the owner and leading architect of his own firm, works in his office with his colleagues. Christian is supported by his wife, Sabina, who is the devoted mother of my two lovely grandchildren, Till Sebastian and Mia Camilla.

Christian asked me to integrate my extensive archive of pictorial and written documents into his office, and a library of 4,000 architecture books has now been installed there. I have never regretted my decision to close my office I had run in Basel for forty years in 2008 and to join a young team of thirty architects in an office in Basel that offered an excellent infrastructure. This change and my contact with such an active group of people have done me the world of good. It is in the nature of change that one emerges reborn. It is only in the context of thinking anew and being active in the here and now where I feel capable of solving the challenges that lie before me. My photographic material preserves my memories and is now situated in a worthy location, one where an active generation of architects is doing meaningful work.

Heim ist Heimat

Heimat ist Heim und Geheimnis – oder: Heimat ist da, wo das Geheimnis wohnt. Dort erlebt und spürt man, was verbindet. Das echte Selbstbewusstsein von meinen eigenen Fähigkeiten bekam ich von meinen Eltern, und dafür bin ich ihnen zeitlebens dankbar. Das Zuhause ist das Sesshafte, ein Ort, wo man hingehört. Aus Goethes Faust: „Was du ererbt von deinen Vätern hast, erwirb es, um es zu besitzen."

Die Direktheit, Aufrichtigkeit und Bereitschaft, Dinge ohne Umschweife zu sagen, habe ich vom Elternhaus übernommen. Mein Vater Gottfried war am Ende seiner Karriere ein Polizeioffizier. Er war stets bemüht, mich in allen Fragen der Entwicklung mit dem bestmöglichen Freiheitsgrad zu begleiten. Ähnlich war meine Mutter Katharina, geschmackvoll in ihren Kleidern und Hausrat. Sie vermittelte mir, ein gesundes Leben zu führen und es in einem positiven Geist zu vollziehen. Mein Vater hingegen war die Stille. Obwohl Geld nie ein Problem war, musste wegen der vier Kinder sparsam damit umgegangen werden.

Ein großes Glück meines Lebens war, dass meine Frau Helen als Textilgestalterin ihre Werke in mein Schaffen integrierte. Als Leiterin der Textilfachklasse an der Gewerbeschule Basel (heute University of Applied Sciences) war sie mit ihrer Handarbeit der gewobenen Bildteppiche prädestiniert, meine Bauten mit Kunst zu beleben. So gab es am Anfang meiner Bürotätigkeit im Atelier, und später im Haus in Bottmingen, einen Webstuhl. Dadurch wurde mir der Zusammenhang von Technik und Kunst plastisch nahegebracht. Das Wort Technik, vom griechischen Wort Techne für handwerkliche Kunstfertigkeit, bedeutet ja auch Kunst: Hinter dem Wesen der Technik steht die Kunst. Das Œuvre von Helen Blaser hat unser Sohn Christian, nach ihrem Tod im Jahr 2004, als Ausstellung in seinem Büro präsentiert. Eingeladen waren ihre und unsere Freunde sowie ehemalige Studentinnen mit der Bitte, sich Objekte ihres Werkes als Erinnerung auszusuchen und mitzunehmen. Mit diesem Geschenk haben wir erreicht, dass ihre Textilkunst erhalten bleibt und weiterwirkt.

Die Geschichte meines Lebens ist erst dann vollständig, wenn ich von unserem Sohn Christian spreche: Wir Eltern haben ihn zum Spielen erzogen, weniger zum Lernen. Doch im Spielen liegt Planung und Aufbau und am Ende des Spiels kommt der ebenso wichtige Teil des Aufräumens, damit ein Neuanfang gewährleistet ist. Aufbau und Einordnen gehören zusammen. Dieses „Spielen" wiederholt sich nun täglich, wenn er mit talentierten Frauen und Männern, als Inhaber und geschäftsführender Architekt seiner Firma, in seinem Büro arbeitet. Auch seine Frau Sabina ist in allen Belangen fördernd. Zugleich lebt sie für die Erziehung meiner beiden Enkel Till Sebastian und Mia Camilla und das Wohl der Familie.

Christian hat mich gebeten, mein großes Archiv von bildnerischen und geistigen Dokumenten in sein Büro zu integrieren. Die Bibliothek von 4.000 Architekturbüchern ist inzwischen in seinen Büroräumen eingerichtet. Es war eine gute Entscheidung, mein großartiges, seit fast 40 Jahren in der St. Alban-Vorstadt in Basel bestehendes Atelier aufzugeben, um im Frühjahr 2008 in ein junges Team mit 30 Architekten und vollständiger Infrastruktur an der Austrasse 24 in Basel einzusteigen. Noch keinen Tag habe ich diese Umsiedlung bereut. Im Gegenteil: Man besitzt, was man zurücklässt. Die Veränderung und der Kontakt zu aktiven Menschen tun mir gut. Änderungen haben es an sich, dass man wie neu geboren wird. Nur im immer wieder neuen, gegenwärtigen Denken und Tun kann ich die herankommenden Anforderungen lösen, und das Fotomaterial bleibt Erinnerung und lagert an einem würdigen Ort, wo eine lebendige Architekturgeneration ihre sinnvolle Arbeit tut.

Peter Zumthor: Gugalun House with new extension, Switzerland, 1990–1994 (photo 2000)
Tomsk, log buildings, 19th century (photo 2000)

Peter Zumthor: Haus Gugalun bei Versam, Schweiz, mit neuentwickeltem Strick, 1990–1994 (Foto 2000)
Tomsk, Blockhausbauten, 19. Jahrhundert (Foto 2000)

Making a Heritage one's Own

My work as a furniture designer, architect, and writer has, of course, been shaped by the different milestones making up my professional biography: a trainee with Alvar Aalto at Artek in Helsinki (1948–1951); studies at the Institute of Design at the Illinois Institute of Technology (1952–1953); research in Japan on the theme of the "contemporary meaning of the temple and tea house" followed by a comprehensive publication (1953); work with Mies van der Rohe in Chicago while working on the publication, *The Art of Structure* (1963 and 1964); guest lecturer at the Ulm School of Design (1956–1957), the University of Pennsylvania in Philadelphia (1978), and the Vienna University of Applied Arts (1983–1984); curating the travelling exhibition "Meaning in Mies van der Rohe's Legacy" in two parts, "Mies Chicago High" and "Work Werner Blaser" at the Berlin University of the Arts (2013); and finally, the "Departure to New Horizons" exhibition of my photo collages to mark my ninetieth birthday in the exhibition space at Blaser Architekten in Basel.

However, these milestones do not reveal much about the formation of the self in the course of a lifetime. From 1948 until his death, the theologian Adolf E. H. Jacob from Lörrach remained one of my closest friends. He was part of my search for myself in all the phases of my development. Adolf was not someone who traded in knowledge, but was certainly a master of dialog and continued to challenge himself throughout his life. His words came from profound thought and experience. It was with him that I was able to discover the essence of world architecture following my six years of travel: the world in its totality and meaningful work within it, which for me was building and design. Discussions with him were a shared process of thinking and rethinking that gave rise to a feeling of self and of togetherness.

Due to my intensive engagement with the legacy of Mies, my own work emerged as a guide to his legacy. In Chicago, I learned from Mies what architecture is really about. I set my own standards and followed my intuition – the certainty that came from my feeling of self-worth. The books I have produced document my understanding of architecture. My photo collages are intended to offer new perspectives on visible construction.

A highpoint of my career was my travelling exhibition focusing on the theme of "Meaning in Mies van der Rohe's Legacy," which was comprised of two parts, "Mies Chicago High" and "Work Werner Blaser," launched at the Berlin University of the Arts in May 2013. The launch was accompanied by an exhibition of my furniture and the production of the film, *Mies Chicago High*. The project was a collaboration with the furniture manufacturer Werner Löffler, whose firm is based near Nuremburg and his consultant, Fritz Močnik. We analyzed what had emerged from Mies's legacy and considered the possible future development of these impulses. A short time prior to this, I was offered an opportunity by the gallery owner, Robert Mertens and his team in Aachen to exhibit photo collages for the first time. The exhibition was held in the Lange and Esters houses in Krefeld, red-brick houses built by Mies in 1928, prior to his emigration to America.

The starting point for these projects was a conversation with Wita Noack, director of the Lemke House designed by Mies in eastern Berlin. It was initially her idea to combine "Mies Chicago High" with "Work Werner Blaser," as she felt that the latter represented a realization of Mies's legacy. Indeed, this was precisely my motivation in the 1953, when I conceived the construction detail as the "art of the joint." The visible joint and connection as a feature of construction is my invention and it has become an established conceptual framework. The exhibition, the film, and also this book ultimately constitute a reflection of my work and my contribution to the creation of meaning and form.

Aus dem Erbe wird Eigenes

Mein Werk als Möbelentwickler Architekt und Publizist ist natürlich geprägt von den Stationen meiner beruflichen Biografie: Praktikant bei Alvar Aalto bei Artek in Helsinki (1948–1951); Studien am Illinois Institute of Technology, The Institute of Design (1952–1953); Recherchen in Japan: Thema „Gegenwartsbedeutung von Tempel und Teehaus“ mit Abschluss einer umfangreichen Publikation (1953); Begegnung und Arbeit mit Mies van der Rohe in Chicago am Werk „Die Kunst der Struktur“ (1963 und 1964); Gastdozent an der Hochschule für Gestaltung in Ulm (1956–1957), der University of Pennsylvania in Philadelphia (1978) und der Universität für angewandte Kunst in Wien (1983–1984); Wanderausstellung „Sinnfindung im Erbe von Mies van der Rohe“ mit Teil 1 „Mies Chicago High“ und Teil 2 „Werk Werner Blaser“ an der Universität der Künste in Berlin (2013); Ausstellung meiner Fotocollagen „Aufbruch zu neuen Horizonten“ zum neunzigsten Geburtstag 2014 im Schauraum bei Blaser Architekten, Basel.

Doch sagen diese Stationen noch wenig darüber aus, wie sich die Selbstbildung in einem solchen Leben gestaltet. Einer meiner wohlgesinnten und alten Freunde war seit 1948 der Theologe Adolf E. H. Jacob aus Lörrach. Auf der Suche nach dem eigenen Ich war er in allen Phasen meiner Entwicklung beteiligt. Er war kein Wissensdealer, wohl aber ein Meister im Dialog, auch mit sich selbst. Seine Worte kamen aus der Tiefe des Denkens und Erlebens. Mit ihm konnte ich nach meiner sechsjährigen Reise das Wesentliche der Weltarchitektur entdecken: die Welt in ihrer Ganzheit und darin die beseelte Arbeit, für mich – des Bauens und Gestaltens. Das Gespräch mit ihm war ein gemeinsames Mitdenken und Umdenken: Es stellte sich ein Selbst- und zugleich ein Wir-Gefühl ein.

Durch meine intensive Auseinandersetzung mit dem Erbe von Mies ist mein eigenes Werk wie ein Wegweiser entstanden. Bei ihm in Chicago lernte ich, worum es in der Architektur geht. Ich folgte meinen eigenen Maßstäben und meiner Intuition – meiner Gewissheit, die aus dem Selbstwertgefühl kommt. Nun liegt mein publizistisches Werk vor, das einem dokumentarischen Architekturverständnis verpflichtet ist. Darüber hinaus sollen meine Fotocollagen neue Perspektiven auf die sichtbare Konstruktion eröffnen.

Ein Höhepunkt war für mich meine Wanderausstellung zum Thema „Sinnfindung im Erbe von Mies van der Rohe“ mit Teil 1 „Mies Chigaco High“ und Teil 2 „Werk Werner Blaser“, die im Mai 2013 in der Universität der Künste in Berlin startete. Dazu wurde eine Serie meiner Möbel ausgestellt und auch ein Film „Mies Chicago High“ produziert. Es war eine Zusammenarbeit mit dem Möbelhersteller Werner Löffler aus Reichenschwand bei Nürnberg und seinem Berater Fritz Močnik. Wir analysierten, was aus dem Erbe von Mies entstanden ist und wie sich die Entwicklung weiter gestalten könnte. Kurz davor konnte ich erstmals meine Fotocollagen auf Einladung des Galeristen Robert Mertens aus Aachen und seines Künstlerteams ausstellen: in den Häusern Lange und Esters in Krefeld, die von Mies 1928 in rotem Backstein gebaut wurden.

Ausgangspunkt zu diesen Projekten war ein Gespräch mit Wita Noack, Leiterin des Hauses Lemke von Mies in Ostberlin. Sie sagte mir, zu „Mies Chicago High“ gehöre auch das „Werk Werner Blaser“, denn darin sei das Erbe Mies verwirklicht. In der Tat: Aus dieser Motivation kreierte ich 1953 das Detail als „Kunst der Fuge“. Das sichtbare Fügen und Verbinden von Konstruktionsteilen ist meine Erfindung, und sie wurde zu einer geistigen Ordnung. Die Ausstellung, der Film und auch dieses Buch sind letztlich eine Reflexion des eigenen Schaffens, meines Beitrags zur Sinn- und Gestaltfindung.

Katsura Imperial Villa, Kyoto, Japan, 1602, Shokin-tei garden teahouse (photo 1953)
Mies van der Rohe: hanging exhibition walls, National Gallery, Berlin, 1962–1968 (photo 2010)

Kaiserliche Katsura-Villa, Kyoto, Japan, 1602, Gartenteehaus Shôkin-tei (Foto 1953)
Mies van der Rohe: Hängende Ausstellungswände, Nationalgalerie Berlin, 1962–1968 (Foto 2010)

Synthesis

It is a great gift to be able to pass on one's life experiences to one's fellow human beings. A healthy life lived without any regret is the basis of this book. In 1963, in Chicago, Mies van der Rohe recommended a book to me. I had been expecting him to name an important architectural tome, but surprisingly he suggested I read *Educating toward Humility* by the Dutch anthropologist and psychologist F. J. J. Buytendijk. Reading it was a very strengthening experience: self-discipline is a path to freedom. Being humble is the ethos of someone who serves, which includes acting, grasping with one's hands, and doing something tangible. It is this ethos that brought me to my craft, guided the development of my tactile sense, and has shaped me to the present day.

What differentiates old age apart from the decline of one's powers? For those who live and have lived with a focus on being themselves, the answer to this question certainly includes a sense of inwardness and composure. In old age, one can still look at the world with open eyes. But rather than always seeing new possibilities, one's relationship to the world is dominated by a sense that there is still a wealth of past experience to be processed. Since the death of my wife, I have lived alone. Our walls used to feature her textile art; today they display my collages.

The last fundamental changes to my way of working and living have entailed shifting from a one-man office, to a large firm and from my house in the country, to an apartment in the city. These changes were suggestions by my son, Christian. I owe him a great debt of gratitude, particularly for the gift of being able to pursue my work on a daily basis at Blaser Architekten. My sincere thanks also go to my assistant, Hélène Felix, who has shown great devotion to this project and who has dealt so conscientiously with my paperwork.

In the fifth century BC, the Greek poet Pindar formulated a sage motto for the way we should pursue our path through life, "Become what you are." I have endeavored to my best ability to discern my own nature and to follow my inner purpose.

Synthesis

Es ist ein großes Geschenk, interessierten Mitmenschen Lebenserfahrungen weitergeben zu können. Ein gesundes Leben, gelebt ohne Wenn und Aber, ist die Basis dieser Niederschrift. In Chicago empfahl mir 1963 Ludwig Mies van der Rohe ein Buch. Eigentlich erwartete ich einen großen Architekturtitel, doch es hatte den Titel „Erziehung zur Demut" (1928), sein Autor war der holländische Anthropologe und Psychologe F. J. J. Buytendijk. Die Lektüre hat mich durchaus gestärkt: Selbstdisziplin ist ein Weg zur Freiheit. Demütig zu sein, ist die Gesinnung eines Dienenden. Dazu gehört aber auch das Handeln, das mit den Händen Fassen, etwas tun. So kam ich zum Handwerk, mein Tastsinn entfaltete sich, er hat mich bis heute geprägt.

Man kann die Frage stellen, was denn im Alter so anders ist außer dem Rückgang der Kräfte. Wer das Sich-selbst-Sein lebt und gelebt hat, stellt nun Innerlichkeit und Gelassenheit in den Vordergrund. Man kann weiterhin mit offenen Augen in die Welt blicken. Aber anstatt immer wieder Neues zu sehen, gilt es jetzt, noch viel Erlebtes zu verarbeiten. Seit dem Tod meiner Frau lebe ich allein. Früher war ihre Textilkunst an den Wänden, heute sind es meine Collagen.

Meine letzten wesentlichen Änderungen beim Arbeiten und beim Wohnen waren: vom Ein-Mann- ins Großbüro, vom Landhaus in die Stadtwohnung. Diese Vorschläge stammten von meinem Sohn Christian. Ihm gehört mein aufrichtiger Dank, insbesondere für das große Geschenk, welches mir dadurch zufällt: meine tägliche Tätigkeit bei Blaser Architekten. Bei meiner Assistentin Hélène Felix, die mit Liebe zur Sache bei diesem Buchprojekt mithalf und meinen Büroarbeiten nachging, bedanke ich mich aufrichtig.

Einem Wort des griechischen Lyrikers Pindar im 5. Jahrhundert. v. Chr. zufolge ist das Motto für unseren Weg zum Ziel: „Werde der du bist." Mein Wesen habe ich zu erkennen und meiner inneren Bestimmung zu folgen versucht.

Temple of Athena, Aphaia, Aegina, Greece, 5th century BCE (photo 1952)
Mies van der Rohe: steel support, National Gallery, Berlin, 1962–1968 (photo 1968)

Tempel der Athene, Aphaia, Ägina, Griechenland, 5. Jahrhundert v. Chr. (Foto 1952)
Mies van der Rohe: Nationalgalerie Berlin, 1962–1968 (Foto 1968)

Amber Fort in Jaipur, Rajasthan, India, 16th century (photo 2010)
Josef Kalous/Jaroslav Valenta, Brno Exhibition Center, Czech Republic, 1927/28 (photo 2010)

Amber-Fort-Palast in Jaipur, Rajasthan, Indien, 16. Jahrhundert (Foto 2010)
Josef Kalous/Jaroslav Valenta, Messegelände Brünn, Tschechien, 1927/28 (Foto 2010)

Epilog
Nachwort

Over the past years, friends have often urged me to write about my many encounters throughout the world. After discussing what could be a suitable title for such a book with my son, Christian, we decided on Synthesis, since this is a book that combines accounts of my experiences with my photo collages.

As a record of my visual experiences and encounters during my travels around the world, this book also enables me to document my understanding of architecture and to reveal what it can achieve in both intellectual and qualitative respects. I have seen great achievements in the course of my life, which have shaped my thinking and my work and have revealed to me the beauty of which architecture is capable.

For this reason, I am pleased that my collected books, texts, plans, and photographs are preserved in the Living Archive maintained by Blaser Architekten AG in Basel, where they will be available for future generations to access. What I have written down here captures moments that remain in memory and that hold the promise for me in my advanced years that life can be reinvented anew.

Immer wieder wurde ich von guten Freunden gebeten, meine vielen weltweiten Begegnungen aufzuschreiben. Im Gespräch mit meinem Sohn Christian über den Buchtitel kamen wir auf „Synthesis“: Gewählt haben wir das Wort, weil dieses Buch die Zusammenführung meiner Erlebnisse mit meinen Fotocollagen darstellt.

Nun kann ich mit diesem Werk, das mein Sehen und meine Begegnungen auf meinen Weltreisen festhält, mein Architekturverständnis dokumentieren, das Machbare in der Architektur aufdecken, in geistiger wie in qualitativer Hinsicht. Großes ist in meinem Lebensrhythmus geschehen, das mein Denken und Machen geprägt und zugleich das Schöne in der Architektur aufbewahrt hat.

Es ist deshalb gut, dass meine gesammelten Bücher, Texte, Pläne und Fotografien als nutzbare Informationen und Materialien im „Living Archive“ bei Blaser Architekten AG aufbewahrt und den nächsten Generationen überlassen werden. Das hier Niedergeschriebene hält Momente fest, die mir in Erinnerung bleiben und mich in meinem Alter zugleich als Verheißung eines neu zu erfindenden Lebens aufmuntern.

Index
Namensregister

Books by
Bücher von Werner Blaser

Tempel und Teehaus in Japan,
Urs Graf, Olten 1955
2. Auflage / 2nd edition
Birkhäuser, Basel 1988

Temples et Jardins au Japon,
Albert Morancé, Paris 1956
Japanese Temples and Tea-Houses,
F. W. Dodge Corp., New York 1956

Wohnen und Bauen in Japan /
Classical Dwelling Houses in Japan,
Arthur Niggli, Niederteufen 1958
2. Auflage / 2nd edition
Niggli, Sulgen 2005

Struktur und Gestalt in Japan,
Artemis, Zürich 1963
Structure and Form in Japan,
Wittenborn & Co., New York 1963

Mies van der Rohe –
Die Kunst der Struktur /
L'Art de la Structure,
Artemis, Zürich 1965
6., überarbeitete und erweiterte Auflage /
6th, revised and enlarged edition
Birkhäuser, Basel 1997

Mies van der Rohe –
The Art of Structure,
Praeger Publishers, New York 1965
2. Auflage / 2nd edition
The Whitney Library of Design,
New York 1993

Mies van der Rohe –
El Arte de la Estructura,
Carlos Hirsch, Buenos Aires 1965

Paperback:
Mies van der Rohe –
Die Kunst der Struktur,
– Artemis, Zürich 1972
– Thames & Hudson, London 1972
– Gustavo Gili, Barcelona 1973
– japanische Ausgabe /
Japanese edition,
A. D. A. Edita, Tokyo 1976
– italienische Ausgabe /
Italian edition,
Zanichelli, Bologna 1977
– niederländische Ausgabe /
Dutch edition,
Uitgeverij, Rotterdam 1986
– portugiesische Ausgabe /
Portugese edition,
Martins Fontes, São Paulo 1994

Objektive Architektur –
Beispiel „Skin and Skeleton"/
Objective Architecture –
Example „Skin and Skeleton",
Richard Scherpe, Krefeld 1970

Chinesische Pavillon-Architektur /
Chinese Pavillon Architecture,
Arthur Niggli, Niederteufen 1974

Strukturale Architektur aus Osteuropa /
Structural Architecture of Eastern Europe,
Zbinden, Basel 1975

Der Fels ist mein Haus /
Le rocher est ma demeure /
The Rock is My Home,
Wepf, Basel 1976

Struktur und Textur /
Structure and Texture,
Richard Scherpe, Krefeld 1976

Prinzip einer Architektur –
Retrospektive 25 Jahre Werner Blaser,
Bündner Kunstmuseum, Chur 1977

Mies van der Rohe – Lehre und Schule /
Principles and School,
Birkhäuser, Basel 1977

Mies van der Rohe – After Mies,
Teaching and Principles,
Van Nostrand Reinhold Company,
New York 1977

Mies van der Rohe – Continuing
the Chicago School of Architecture,
2., erweiterte Auflage /
2nd, enlarged edition
Birkhäuser, Basel 1981

Holz Haus / Maisons de bois /
Wood Houses,
Wepf, Basel 1980
2., erweiterte Auflage /
2nd, enlarged edition 1985

Filigran Architektur/
Architecture en filigrane /
Filigree Architecture,
Wepf, Basel 1980

Hofhaus in China /
Courtyard House in China,
Birkhäuser, Basel 1979
2., erweiterte Auflage /
2nd, enlarged edition 1995

Mies van der Rohe
Il design di Mies van der Rohe,
Electa Editrice, Milano 1980
– Furniture and Interiors,
Academy Editions, London 1980
– Les Maîtres du Design,
Electa Moniteur, Paris 1980
– Möbel und Interieurs, Deutsche
Verlags-Anstalt, Stuttgart 1981

Il design di Alvar Aalto,
Electa Editrice, Milano 1981
Alvar Aalto als Designer,
Deutsche Verlags-Anstalt, Stuttgart 1982

Architecture 70/80 in Switzerland,
Birkhäuser, Basel 1981
2., erweiterte Auflage /
2nd, enlarged edition 1983
Textausgaben: deutsch, français,
italiana, español, portuguesa
Architecture 70/80 in Switzerland
Birkhäuser, Basel 1982

Architecture 70/80 in Switzerland,
compendious presentation, 1983
(English, Français, Epañol)
Birkhäuser, Basel 1983

Klappstühle / Folding Chairs,
Birkhäuser, Basel 1982

Elementare Bauformen /
Elemental Building Forms,
Beton, Düsseldorf 1982

Schweizer Holzbrücken /
Ponts de Bois en Suisse
Wooden Bridges in Switzerland,
Birkhäuser, Basel 1982

Bauernhaus der Schweiz,
Birkhäuser, Basel 1983

Drawings of Great Buildings /
Zeichnungen Grosser Bauten,
Birkhäuser, Basel 1983

Architecture and Nature –
the work of Alfred Caldwel l /
Architecture et Nature –
l'oeuvre d'Alfred Caldwel l /
Architektur und Natur –
das Werk von Alfred Caldwell,
Birkhäuser, Basel 1984

Element – System – Möbel,
Deutsche Verlags-Anstalt, Stuttgart 1984

Atrium-Lichthöfe, fünf Jahrtausende /
Open courtyards 5000 years,
Wepf, Basel 1985

Architektur im Möbel /
Furniture as Architecture,
Waser, Zürich 1985

Mies van der Rohe – less is more,
Waser, Zürich 1986

Fantasie in Holz / Fantasy in Wood,
Birkhäuser, Basel 1987

Myron Goldsmith – Bauten und Konzepte /
Buildings and Concepts,
Birkhäuser, Basel 1987
Rizzoli, New York 1987

China – Tao in der Architektur/
Tao in Architecture
mit C. K. Chang,
Birkhäuser, Basel 1987

Tao – Architecture de Chine
avec C. K. Chang,
André Delcourt, Lausanne 1988

Tempel und Teehaus in Japan /
Temple and Tea-House in Japan,
neue Auflage / new edition
Birkhäuser, Basel 1988

Santiago Calatrava, Ingenieur-Architektur / Engineering Architecture, Birkhäuser, Basel 1988
2., erweiterte Auflage / 2nd, enlarged edition 1990
span.-engl. Lizenzausgabe, Gustavo Gili, Barcelona 1989

Richard Meier, Building for Art / Bauen für die Kunst, Birkhäuser, Basel 1990

Tadao Ando Sketches / Zeichnungen, Birkhäuser, Basel 1990

Ernst Koller 1900–1990, Kontraste eines Konstrukteurs, Krebs, Basel 1990

Norman Foster-Sketches, Birkhäuser, Basel 1991

Helmut Jahn – Airports, Birkhäuser, Basel 1991

Bauen vor der Stadt / Suburban Building mit Dieter Wronsky, Birkhäuser, Basel 1991

Orient / Occident, Beton, Düsseldorf 1991

Fügen – Verbinden / Joint – Connection das Werk von / the work of Werner Blaser, Birkhäuser, Basel 1992

Chicago Architecture – Holabird & Root 1880–1992, Birkhäuser, Basel 1992

Richard Meier, Weishaupt Forum, Birkhäuser, Basel 1993

Norman Foster, Sketch Book, Birkhäuser, Basel 1993

Mies van der Rohe – Die Kunst der Struktur, neue Auflage Birkhäuser, Basel 1992

Mies van der Rohe – The Art of Structure, new Edition The Whitney Library of Design, New York 1993

Tomsk – Textur in Holz / Texture in wood / Texture en bois, Birkhäuser, Basel 1993

Livio Vacchini-Transformation, Birkhäuser, Basel 1994

Restaurants Paris Belle Epoque, Waser, Zürich 1995

Richard Horden – light tech, Birkhäuser, Basel 1995

Metall Pionier Architektur / Metal Pioneer Architecture, Waser, Zürich 1995

Holz Pionier Architektur / Wood Pioneer Architecture, Waser, Zürich 1996

Stein Pionier Architektur / Stone Pioneer Architecture, Waser, Zürich 1996

Helmut Jahn Transparency / Transparenz, Birkhäuser, Basel 1996

West Meets East – Mies van der Rohe, Birkhäuser, Basel 1996
2., erweiterte Auflage / 2nd, enlarged edition 2001

Richard Meier, Details, Birkhäuser, Basel 1996

Mies van der Rohe Studio Paperback, Birkhäuser, Basel 1997

patios – 5000 años de evolución, Gustavo Gili, Barcelona 1997

Renzo Piano – Museum Beyeler, Benteli, Bern 1998

Werner Sobek Ingenieur-Kunst / Art of Engineering, Birkhäuser, Basel 1999

Mies van der Rohe, Farnsworth House, Birkhäuser, Basel 1999

Mies van der Rohe, Lake Shore Drive Apartments, Birkhäuser, Basel 1999

Tadao Ando Museum der Weltkulturen im Rhein, Vice Versa, Berlin 1999

West is East is West, Mies van der Rohe, Vice Versa, Berlin 2000

Ernst Koller – Erfinder und Konstrukteur Investor and Designer at the age of 100 years, Wepf, Basel 2000

Begegnungen mit Werner Blaser An Architect meets Architects, Birkhäuser, Basel 2000

Nelly Rudin innen ist aussen / inside is outside, Offizin, Zürich 2000

Christa de Carouge habit habitat, German / French / English Editions Lars Müller, Baden 2000

Mies van der Rohe IIT Crown Hall, Birkhäuser, Basel 2001

Ernst Koller, Leben – Wohnen, Wepf, Basel 2001

Tadao Ando-Architektur der Stille / Architecture of Silence, Birkhäuser, Basel 2001

Powell / Kleinschmidt Interior Architecture, Birkhäuser, Basel 2001

Renzo Piano – Centre Kanak, Birkhäuser, Basel 2002

Kurt Brägger, Zoo Basel, Reinhardt, Basel 2002

Werner Sobek, R 128 Bauen im 21. Jahrhundert / Architecture in the 21st century, Birkhäuser, Basel 2002

Natur im Gebauten / Nature in Building Rudolf Steiner in Dornach, Birkhäuser, Basel 2002

Klaus Schuldt / Andreas Scheiwiller Ensemble Habitat, Birkhäuser, Basel 2002

Mies van der Rohe IIT Campus, Birkhäuser, Basel 2002

Helmut Jahn Architecture / Engineering, Birkhäuser, Basel 2002

Helmut Jahn Bayer Konzernzentrale, Birkhäuser, Basel 2003

Souto de Moura Element Stein / Element Stone, Birkhäuser, Basel 2003

Gene Summers Art / Architecture, Birkhäuser, Basel 2003

Helmut Jahn Post Tower Bonn, Birkhäuser, Basel 2003

Innen-Hof / Courtyards in Marrakech, Birkhäuser, Basel 2004

Theo Hotz – Weishaupt / CH, Niggli, Sulgen 2004

Mies van der Rohe Federal Center, Birkhäuser, Basel 2004

patios – 5000 anños de evolución, 2nd edition Gustavo Gili, Barcelona 2004
Wilhelm Münger Geist im Holz / Spirit in wood, Reinhardt, Basel 2004

Helmut Jahn State Street Village IIT, Flash Press, Chicago 2004

Japan Wohnen + Bauen / Dwelling Houses, Niggli, Sulgen 2005

Jakob Schilling Planen Bauen, Sturm, Muttenz 2005

Renzo Piano Zentrum Paul Klee, German / French / English editions Reinhardt, Basel 2005

Tadao Ando Nähe des Fernen / The Nearness of the Distant, Niggli, Sulgen 2005

Werner Blaser Passion eines Lebens / Passion of a Life, Sturm, Muttenz 2006

Tadao Ando Bauen in die Erde / Sunken Courts, Niggli, Sulgen 2007

Archi Swiss Parallelen mit der Grossen Welt, Regent, Basel 2009

Im Garten Isfahan In the garden of Isfahan, Niggli, Sulgen 2009

Ikonen der Weltarchitektur / Icons of World Architecture, Niggli, Sulgen 2012

Zen Teehaus / Teahouse, Elster, Zürich 2012

Sinnfindung im Erbe Mies Mies Chicago High, Löffler, Reichenschwand 2013

Sinnfindung im Erbe Mies Werk Werner Blaser / at Work, Löffler, Reichenschwand 2013

Translation from German into English: Joseph O'Donnell
English copy editing: Anna Roos
Project management: Lisa Schulze
Production: Heike Strempel
Layout: Christian Blaser, Hélène Felix
Typesetting: Sven Schrape
Cover design: Kathleen Bernsdorf
Paper: ProfiMatt 170 g/m²
Printing: DZA Druckerei zu Altenburg GmbH

Library of Congress Cataloging-in-Publication data
A CIP catalog record for this book has been applied for at the Library of Congress.

Bibliographic information published by the German National Library
The German National Library lists this publication in the Deutsche Nationalbibliografie; detailed bibliographic data are available on the Internet at http://dnb.dnb.de.

This publication is also available as an e-book
(ISBN PDF 978-3-0356-0951-6; ISBN EPUB 978-3-0356-0945-5).

P.O. Box 44, 4009 Basel, Switzerland
Part of Walter de Gruyter GmbH, Berlin/Boston

Printed on acid-free paper produced from chlorine-free pulp. TCF ∞

Printed in Germany

ISBN 978-3-0356-1136-6

9 8 7 6 5 4 3 2 1 www.birkhauser.com